Journeys in Bohemia's Inspired Landscapes
The Baroque Statues by the Patzak Family of Sculptors

IMPRINT

Heinz Patzak, Werner Honal Editors
www.baroko-pak.eu

© 2023 the editors
All rights reserved

PRINTING AND DISTRIBUTION ON BEHALF OF THE EDITORS:

Europe
Buchschmiede by Dataform Media GmbH, Vienna
Book order at: www.buchschmiede.at

978-3-99165-063-8 *(Paperback)*
978-3-99165-062-1 *(E-Book)*

USA and worldwide
Ordering information at:
www.baroko-pak.eu

Front cover:
St. John Nepomuk, Georg F. Patzak, Nedielischt (Neděliště)

Journeys in Bohemia's Inspired Landscapes

The Baroque Statues by the Patzak Family of Sculptors

HEINZ PATZAK
WERNER HONAL
EDITORS

St Mary, Georg F. Patzak, Chrudim MuBaSa

Text by

Jan Cisař
Vojtěch Berger
Karel Dolista
Cynthia Fontayne
Hana Hadas
Tomáš Hladik
Gerhard Honal
Werner H. Honal
Ignác A. Hrdina
David Junek
Ludmila Kesselgruberová
Ivo Kořán
Marie-Christine Leitgeb
Heinz Patzak
Peter Patzak
Zdenka Paukrtová
Jan Pipek
Stephan Sweerts-Sporck

Bernhard Patzak

We editors would have liked to have included portraits of the Baroque sculptors Patzak (Pacák) at the front of this book, but we include these two other Patzaks as "placeholders" until research finds a likeness of our earlier ancestors.

From 1736 onwards, Georg F. Patzak (ca. 1670–1742), and his son Franz Patzak (1713–1757), worked not only with sculptors, but also with painters in a private art academy in Moravian Trübau (Moravská Třebová / Mährisch Trübau). Among them was Georg F. Patzak's brother-in-law, Judas Thaddäus Supper (1712–1771), who secretly included friends, family and even himself, in many of his frescoes. Maybe one of the two Patzaks?

There was another Patzak in this history, one who researched the Baroque 150 years after that art period. Prof. Dr. Bernhard Patzak taught art history on the north side of the Giant Mountains, at the University of Breslau (Wrocław) in Lower Silesia (Dolnośląskie). His specialty was the fine art of the Baroque in Silesia. Numerous texts and photos of him have survived, of a member of the large Patzak family. The first pair of Patzak ancestors were probably called to East Bohemia after the Hussite wars (1419–1434) as German Silesians.

Patzak couple,
Breslau (Wrocław)

The picture above shows Bernhard Patzak in Breslau in 1914 with his wife, Monika, née Hochschwarzer.

On 19 October 1912, the couple celebrated the arrival of their only child, Hermann Walter Josef Patzak, whose birth in Liegnitz was recorded with the spelling Patzack by the registrar there. Hermann Patzack; the picture below shows him in a stroller with the proud parents. At his own wedding on August 12, 1944, he was again called Hermann Walter Josef Patzak in the certificate of the German registrar in Breslau, minus the c in his family name.

Patzak family,
Breslau (Wrocław)

Bohemian culture is back

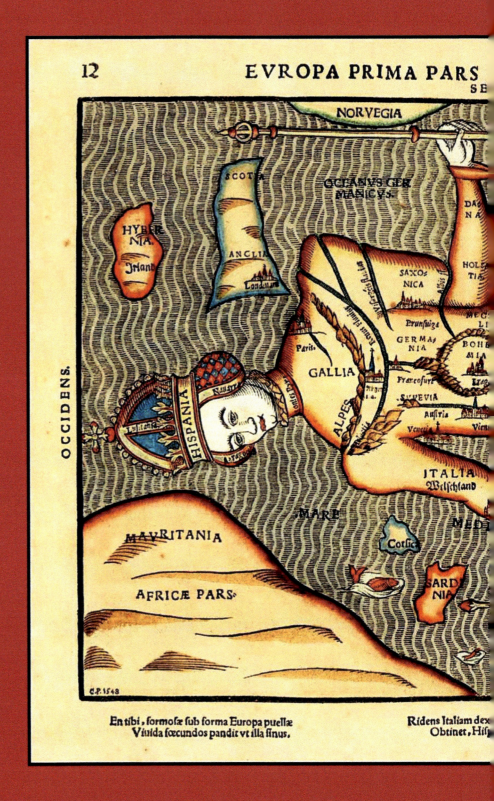

With the "Velvet Revolution" of 1989 and its accession to the European Union in 2004, the Czech Republic has returned to the heart of Europe. Now it is possible to travel to the outstanding works of art that artists from Europe have created in Bohemia and the Czech Republic over the course of a thousand years.

The Baroque period was a Pan-European phenomenon, which encompassed all areas of art and life, and was one of the foundation stones of our European sensibility. This epoch and its art were sovereign beyond political borders existing long before our current ones. This was the opinion of the Tyrolean cartographer Johannes Putsch, who published a map with the attractive title "Europa Regina" ("Europe Queen") in 1537.

in the heart of Europe

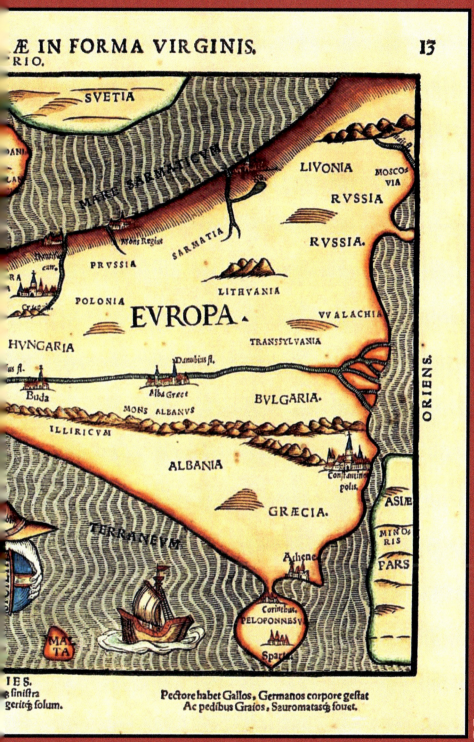

Regina Europa,
Heinrich Pünting

In the map, the head of this Virgin Queen is formed by the Iberian Peninsula, the royal orb by Sicily. However, her heart, which is encircled by laurel, is formed by the Kingdom of Bohemia. Its historic importance, its geographic location, the economic importance of the realm and the cultural diversity of its inhabitants, in which the diversity of all Europe is reflected—all this is symbolized by "Europa Regina". Artists like Georg F. Patzak (Jiří F. Pacák) have transformed with their work not only the landscape, but the European mentality as well. Feeling responsible for the care of these examples of European cultural patrimony is not just for "those at the top". Responsibility for conserving the assets of our culture falls on us all, on each citizen of a country. Today's students should learn about and appreciate these works of art from the Baroque era.

Diana,
Georg F. Patzak,
Leitomschl
(Litomyšl)

In 1999 the castle in Leitomischl (Litomyšl), for whose garden G.F. Patzak created figures of gods, included in the World Heritage List.

Why This Book?

Prof. Dr. Bernd Freiherr von Droste zu Hülshoff, Founding Director of the UNESCO World Heritage Center

The Inspired Landscape of Eastern Bohemia is a book about art history, and it is a book *with* history, and a mission: enabling the renaissance of a unique collection of European art that was thought to have been lost forever.

This spurred Munich-based philologist and genealogist Werner Honal, born in Prague, to begin compiling documentation about the works of this family of artists, while Heinz Patzak, then based in Paris, now in Vienna, began making preparations to publish a comprehensive book about them. I greatly appreciated the interesting and well-sourced information about these master sculptors of Eastern Bohemia, presented by Messrs. Honal and Patzak. Thanks to their collaboration with leading Czech and international art specialists, the quality of their art history research was at a high level right from the start.

The Czech Republic has registered with UNESCO an excellent collection of world heritage sites and additional candidates for this title and honor, a welcome change particularly for those sites and candidates which feature Baroque cultural artifacts. During the Soviet era, Bohemian Baroque art did not fit into the Marxist-Leninist and anti-clerical paradigms, which meant a treasure trove of Czech culture was lost to whole generations of students, and paintings and sculptures were abandoned to decay.

Georg Franz Patzak / Jiří František Pacák (1670–1742), born a serf more than three and a half centuries ago, was a great artist and a fascinating personality of his time, and one of the few Bohemian masters who created both intricate carving work and monumental stone sculptures.

The Inspired Landscape of Eastern Bohemia is the history of a German-Bohemian family of artists and is designed to tell the story of art from the varying perspectives of history, religion, tourism, and human interest, as well as art scholarship.

Georg F. Patzak's life, his works and unique presence in key aspects of Bohemian history offer the perfect narrative context for arousing interest in and understanding the imperative for the restoration and preservation of these priceless works of art.

It is true that the Baroque landscape, which is estimated by the Czech national office of monuments, (NPU), as being a "European unicum", a unique exemplar, has a high priority for restoration. Nevertheless, the budgets are insufficient by far, and the situation remains problematical. And more than money is required; the appreciation and protection of both nature and art require the support and participation of the public.

It is with good reason that the European Commission has chosen sustainable cultural tourism as one of the main pillars of its tourism policy in order to generate income in similar cases, to increase the esteem and respect for works of art, to stop decay and to demonstrate the risks of climate change for humans, nature, and art.

The proven strategy of initiating long-term behavioral change follows three steps, as described by Freeman Tillman, the father of heritage interpretation, **"Through understanding, interpretation; through appreciation, understanding; through appreciation, protection."**

In 2014 the editors started the project "Baroque Patzak" which stands firmly on three legs, this travel book, the website *www.baroko-pak.eu* which offers news on restorations and research, and the third component the upcoming larger and detailed Patzak art history book in German, *East Bohemia's Inspired Landscapes*.

In this travel and art book, the reader will go on a thrilling and enlightening journey to the world of the Baroque sculptors of the Patzak Family, who made a decisive contribution to the design of the cultural landscape of Eastern Bohemia.

It is our sincere hope that this book will enable more people to discover, understand and be inspired by the cultural area of Bohemia and Moravia with its unique Baroque art of building and architecture. This new knowledge will serve the book's ultimate mission: establishing the community and civic will to rescue and preserve works of art.

Prof. Dr. Bernd Freiherr von Droste zu Hülshoff

Contents of the Book

I. The Baroque in Bohemia and the Patzaks — p. 12

I.1 A Search for Clues Takes a Surprising Turn (Werner H. Honal) — p. 14

I.2 Thank You, Count Sporck!
A Journey to the Beginnings of the Patzak Family of Artists (Heinz Patzak) — p. 20

I.3 The Religious Source of Power of the Stilo Moderno (Heinz Patzak) — p. 32

℗ I.4 Born—Being—Perishing—Being—Kukus is Living! (Mag. Sweerts-Sporck) — p. 38

℗ I.5 Joy of Living—Born Out of the Ashes of War (Gerhard Honal) — p. 38

℗ I.6 The Church in Europe is Reformed Three Times (Werner H. Honal) — p. 39

℗ I.7 The Era of the Baroque Sculptors Patzak (W. Honal / H. Patzak) — p. 41

℗ I.8 Carvers of the Viennese Jesuits, Master Braun's Successors (Jan Pipek) — p. 41

℗ I.9 The Source of Creativity of Georg F. Patzak (Peter Patzak) — p. 43

℗ 1.10 The Baroque Drama of Eastern Bohemia (Ivo Kořán) — p. 43

I.11 The Family of Baroque Sculptors Patzak (Werner H. Honal) — p. 44

II. A Closer Look at Some Baroque Artworks — p. 50

℗ II.1 Sculptors—Wood Carvers—Gilders (Zdenka Paukrtová) — p. 52

℗ II.2 The Pietà at Abtsdorf (Opatov) (Ludmilla Kesselgruberová) — p. 54

II.3 Politschka, the Baroque Jewel (David Junek) — p. 55

℗ II.4 Georg F. Patzak in the National Gallery of Prague (Tomáš Hladík) — p. 65

℗ III. 20th Century Echoes — p. 66

℗ III.1 In J. Tejkl's "Calvary". G.F. Patzak as a Stage Hero (Jan Cisař) — p. 68

℗ III.2 G. F. Patzak / J. F. Pacák on Stage (Vojtech Berger) — p. 70

℗ III.3 V. V. Štech is Imprisoned in Dachau and Buchenwald during
the Nazi's "Albrecht I" Campaign (Werner Honal) — p. 71

 is the symbol for the upcoming book about the family of Baroque sculptors Patzak *Bohemia's Inspired Landscape* (*Böhmens beseelte Landschaft*). A few lines in this travel-and-art book on the baroque sculptors Patzak refer to this expanded volume. You can find out more about this future book, including when and where it will be available, at www.baroko-pak.eu or by sending an email to info@baroko-pak.eu.

IV. A Journey Through East Bohemia
Experiencing the Works of Baroque Sculptors Patzak   p. 72
(Vojtěch Berger)

IV.1 Chrudim   p. 74
IV.2 Lusche (Luže)   p. 76
IV.3 Politschka (Policka)   p. 78
IV.4 Unter Aujezd (Dolní Újezd)   p. 80
IV.5 Leitomischl (Litomyšl)   p. 82
IV.6 Moravian Trübau (Moravská Třebová)   p. 84
IV.7 Smirschitz (Smiřice)   p. 86
IV.8 Josefstadt (Josefov Fortress)   p. 88
IV.9 Kukus (Kuks)   p. 90
IV.10 Braun's Bethlehem Sculpture Park (Betlém, nativity scene)   p. 94
IV.11 Schurz (Žireč)   p. 96
IV.12 Dubenetz (Dubenec)   p. 98
IV.13 Qualisch (Chvaleč)   p. 100
IV.14 Schatzlar (Žaclér)   p. 102
IV.15 Hohenelbe (Vrchlabí)   p. 106
IV.16 Prague (Praha)   p. 108

V. Restoration and Preservation   p. 112
V.1 Civic Commitment—an Example at Schurz. Planted into the Landscape (Ignác A. Hrdina)   p. 114
V.2 Ecclesiastical Commitment—Let the Baroque Works of the Patzaks be Viewed (Werner H. Honal)   p. 115
V.3 Municipal Commitment—An Example: St. Florian and Königinhof on the Elbe River (Werner H. Honal)   p. 116
V.4 Commitment of the Patzak relatives alive today (Werner H. Honal)   p. 117

VI. Appendices   p. 118
VI.1 Bibliography   p. 120
VI.2 Indices   p. 120
VI.3 Credits (authors, designers, photographers, sources)   p. 120

VII. Travel Map 16 Destinations   back cover

St. Franz Xaver
Josef or Georg F. Patzak
Schurz (Žirec)

I.

I. The Baroque in Bohemia and the Patzaks

St. Franz Xaver, Josef or Georg F. Patzak, Schurz (Žireč)

I. 1
A Search for Clues Takes a Surprising Turn
(Werner H. Honal)

Sacred Art Preserved in Churches and Outdoor Settings Around East Bohemia
Actually, I wanted to look for the grave of my Czech Patzak grandmother in Könighof an der Elbe (Dvůr Kralove nad Labem) in East Bohemia. I traveled from Dubenetz (Dubenec) to Schurz (Žireč), crossed the Elbe (Labe) and, to my great surprise, encountered near the top of the Mühlberg (hill behind the mill) a large statue that had obviously been restored. This figure of a saint, Francis Xavier, baptizing a child and raising a cross in his left hand towards the east, had a dynamic and expressive power that reminded me of Bernini's Baroque figures in Rome. I had not expected to find anything like that in this place.

My next surprise was that the artist who had created this compelling sculpture shared a surname with my grandparents, who had been living in the vicinity: Patzak. The plaque on the sculpture reads: Jiři František Pacák, in German: Georg Franz Patzak.

Since that first dramatic discovery, the Baroque artists named Patzak have been on my mind. Of primary concern was that many of their works were in danger of falling into fatal disrepair. What could be done to preserve them?

Various circumstances and threats impeded the preservation of works of art made nearly four centuries ago by the sculptors named Patzak in the landscape of Eastern Bohemia:
» acid rain and overgrowth;
» neglect, theft and vandalism;
» ideological reservations and a lack of basic knowledge of the Baroque;
» gaps in research;
» a lack of public awareness.

That statue of St. Francis Xavier used to be so well known and popular that in the 1920s there were even picture postcards of it. In his 1937 regional arts guide, Emanuel Poche cited the sculpture, included a photo of it and attributed it to Josef Patzak, who was the master sculptor of the Jesuits at Schurz, his hometown. As early as that same year, however, the Saint was missing the cross and his gold-plated halo. Weather and acid rain had badly affected the sandstone.

If I had passed by this figure before 2008, I would not have discovered it. Over the course of 60 years, it had become fully overgrown. It was not until 2008 that the Hubertus Order, which is private not ecclesiastical, from neighboring Kukus (Kuks), started to free it from its leafy prison. By September 2012, with strong support from the European Union, the Order had succeeded in restoring St. Francis Xavier.

Could This Be a Model for Rescuing and Restoring Similar Figures?

The particular qualities of these Baroque statues, which are far away from churches and municipal squares, can best be appreciated if they are visited at the sites of their original installation, as the artist had intended that the works be an integral part of the landscape. In 2002, the Czech National Office for the Preservation of Historical Monuments (NPU) announced that approximately 200 Baroque works of art had been found in roadside ditches and landfills. A Czech newspaper commented on this report, "These Baroque figures integrated with the landscape are unique in Europe; cultural treasures like these can only be found in the Czech Republic."

During the era of nationalism and communism, these religious statues were no doubt a disturbing presence, so it is no surprise that they fell victim to neglect. But even today, they remain endangered and mostly unknown by the public. Sadly, after the statue's restoration, St. Francis Xavier once again had his halo stolen.

In the 18th and 19th centuries, the Patzaks were well known for their many masterworks in churches in the region between Leitomischl (Litomyšl) in the south of Eastern Bohemia and Schatzlar (Žacléř) in the north. In Politschka (Polička), the Marian or Plague Column, which was designed by Georg F. Patzak in 1731, is now being restored. It is 22 meters (72 feet) high, resting on a triangular plinth and mounted on three balustrades, just like a pyramid. Experts and laymen agree that this is the most magnificent monument of its kind in the Czech Republic.

Not all these works are endangered, often because it is their duplicates that are standing in the open air. Even in Kukus, the Baroque pearl of the Czech Republic, the original statues are standing indoors, sheltered from the elements. The two dozen replicas, depicting vices and virtues, that are placed outdoors make clear that a powerful impression is created by the way the figures relate to the landscape in which they have been placed. Originally these outdoor figures were painted, which helped to protect them from wind and weather, especially in the days before acid rain.

Most works made by the Patzaks are located in churches, but now, unfortunately, most of these churches must be locked, which means they are safe from vandalism but difficult to be seen by visitors. At the pilgrimage church Mariahilf in Lusche (Luže), at least, an accessible and transparent entrance area has been created, so visitors can see this wonderful early work of Georg F. Patzak, and even that glimpse is absolutely worth the trip.

The history and the creator of this work was discovered in the 1970s in the deteriorating files of the Jesuits in Leitomischl, not by an art expert but by a drama teacher, Josef Tejkl of Königgrätz (Hradec Králové). After the Prague Spring had been suppressed, Tejkl wrote a play about Georg F. Patzak and the sculptor's opposition to the repression by the Jesuits, which was a clever allegory to express Tejkl's opposition to the repressive communist regime in his own time.

A stronger expression emanates from the later works of the Patzaks, which are standing in or around churches in Leitomischl and Schatzlar, and also in the landscape. Before 1990, studying them was difficult for art historians in the former Czechoslovakia; historical materials related to the church had been badly maintained in the archives, and it was not politically expedient to publish studies of the Baroque period. If relevant conferences took place at all, they did so behind closed doors. So, during this period it fell to laymen with an interest in the field of art history, such as Josef Tejkl or Jan Pipek from Hohenelbe (Vrchlabí), to research and expand the archives related to the artistic achievements of the Patzak family.

Professional art historians at that time would rather only deal with certain, mainly technical, details, such as the type of folds of the garments of the statues. In one instance, this led to the assertion that the famous Calvary monument in Mährisch Trübau (Moravská Třebová) was the work of one of Patzak's pupils and not of the master sculptor himself.

In another instance, the appearance of nine of the two dozen figures in the Kukus series depicting vices and virtues, among other things, led art historians Emmanuel Poche and Ivo Kořan from Prague to attribute these works of art to Georg F. Patzak, then a leading member of Matthias Bernhard Braun's workshop. (This attribution has not yet been verified in the archives.)

The Works Created by the Baroque Artists Patzak Are Located in the Province

The later Patzak works include a figure of Saint John of Nepomuk. After a search request made by the National Office for the Preservation of Historical Monuments (NPU), it was found in a ditch near the Castle Park in Dobschenitz (Dobřenice), 10 km (6 miles) west of Königgrätz. Then it was restored temporarily and fittingly put into the landscape again. In spring 2016, I looked for it in vain. After vandals had damaged the statue several times, the bishopric decided to keep it in a wooden box on the locked church property. There the figure will survive, but the artist definitely did not intend this to be its fate. Art can only have an impact if it can actually be seen.

The works created by Josef Patzak, Georg F. Patzak and Franz Patzak are exclusively located in this province, and can be found neither in Brünn (Brno) nor in Prague (Praha). Travel guides and other tourism information are strongly focused on Prague and fail to mention them, which is just one example of the lack of media attention they have received. This is in stark contrast to the works made by their teacher and colleague, Matthias Bernhard Braun, even though Patzak was regarded as Braun's master pupil, who continued his work and even surpassed him. When Václav Havel, the celebrated writer, dissident, and first president of the new Czech Republic, met noted film director Peter Patzak, it was clear that Havel was aware of the artistic legacy of the Baroque-era Patzaks. He said, "You bear the name of a great artist who is known to few Czechs. But this will change."

St. John Nepomuk, Georg F. Patzak, Dobschenitz (Dobrenice)

The conditions necessary to make President Havel's prediction a reality will come only after the population's basic human needs, such as food, shelter and safety, have been satisfied. As Berthold Brecht put it in the *Three Penny Opera*, "Erst kommt das Fressen, dann kommt die Moral," ["First comes food, then comes morality."] Art, too, plays second fiddle.

Background Knowledge Opens Up Art and the Present

Art requires understanding, which in turn requires curiosity. Unfortunately, knowledge of Baroque art and a curiosity for understanding it were not imparted in Czech schools before the political change. The Baroque era did not fit into the Marxist-Leninist view of history. Thus it was treated as if it never existed, even though this was the same era in which essential elements of the Czech language were developed.

Today, the history curriculum rightly presents the Baroque era in a positive light. Yet all those who went to school before 1990, as well as many teachers themselves, will have to work at closing this gap in their knowledge on their own. For example, this knowledge also includes knowing that 95 % of people in the 17th and 18th centuries could not read the written language but definitely knew many elements of imagery and the meaning of the symbols in statues better than we do today. Is it not possible that this imagery makes people curious? Studying the Baroque era, with its great music, poetry and sculptures, is a worthy challenge for adult education and the media in the Czech Republic and elsewhere.

Background knowledge also should include understanding what life and belief systems were like during that period, what the saints meant to them and how we understand the saints today. Saint Agnes of Bohemia had even succeeded in appearing on a banknote in the Czech Republic. Presumably it also is her sanctification that has contributed to the success of the Velvet Revolution. Could the following topics be important topics of today's Roman Catholic Church in the Czech Republic: imagery—symbols—saints? If so, should the Church not utilize all modern media as well? How could the Church fullfill its mission by presenting such topics in social media? Should not art be made more accessible in churches so that Baroque art may appreciated once again?

The Patzaks Were Europeans, at the Same Time Bohemians and Germans

Nowadays young people all over Europe are expressing a new interest in Baroque art and monuments. If such monuments are outside the cities, they also are well suited to serve as landmarks for the modern scavenger hunt via GPS, geocaching. Then the digital accompanying material could, for example, furnish some historical background about St. Francis Xavier at Schurz. Perhaps small groups of young people could be formed and encouraged to take on direct and digital sponsorships of certain Baroque monuments in their respective areas, in the manner of the Hubertus Order in Kukus. Supported by their teachers, municipal officials and the local tourist office, students could promote the landmarks online and even give guided tours. This could be one way that smart phones could prove to be more than high tech toys: they also could be a tool to help secure the future of European culture.

In the Czech archives, quite a lot of material has already been digitized, enhancing the opportunities for art historical research. As for the church register and land registers, this service is at the top worldwide. Archival material that has been hard to access and has not been maintained up to now could be accessed via the internet to clarify the many open questions about the Patzaks. Several bachelor and master theses and a doctoral dissertation have as their subject these Baroque sculptors. In most cases, however, they did not include new findings that can be found in the archives, in contrast to what Tejkl and Pipek did in the 1980s.

Holy Family,
Georg F. Patzak,
Dubenetz (Dubenec)

When basic understanding is there, exhibitions about Baroque art created by the Patzaks can reawaken public passion for this important component of Czech cultural heritage. It is essential that such exhibits be well publicized and supported with information about the works of art created by the Patzaks that also can be admired in Chrudim, in the Museum of The Baroque Sculptures, and in the Prague National Gallery in Schwarzenberg Palace.

In this respect, I would like to note that, in my opinion, it is no solution to dislocate works made by the Patzaks by moving them into museums; they should be positioned in both their open air locations and in churches, as originally conceived and created by the artists.

The call for help published on the internet by the Municipality of Dubenetz, not far from Kukus, is alarming: The sculptures of Georg F. Patzak dated 1740 and presumably his latter work might be ruined if a solution to rescue the church of Saint Joseph is not found soon. Patzak's group of colored sculptures depicting the Holy Family is placed on the high altar there. Government, the tourism industry and the art community can all share responsibility to take steps to preserve this church and its irreplaceable art.

Regional tourism promotion materials should direct visitors to works of art in the local landscape. The German edition of the travel Guide *Baedeker Reiseführer Tschechien*, (*Travel Guide to the Czech Republic*), includes the name of Baroque artist Jiří František Pacák in the section on Eastern Bohemia. The Czech internet, too, has many references to the Baroque artists Pacák. But this is not enough.

An illustrated travel section was prepared by a renowned journalist from Prague. At this writing, however, we are lacking the sponsors that would enable us to start the first edition in German as well as a Czech-language edition, which could be offered at a price that makes it accessible to experts and the general public alike—and could contribute to preserving sacred art with a European dimension in the Czech landscape and to enhancing understanding among nations in Europe. The Patzaks were quintessentially Bohemian, both German and Czech, bilingual, and at home in both cultures. So they are a perfect example of how national conflicts can be clarified and resolved from a European perspective. It is our intention and hope that our book also will make a contribution to this reconciliation and international cooperation.

I.2
Thank You, Count Sporck! A Journey to the Beginnings of the Patzak Family of Artists
(Heinz Patzak)

Count Franz A. von Sporck Seemed Like a Glimpse Into the Future

In his 1998 book *How Chance Writes World History*[1], Austrian writer Karl Durschmied reviews case studies whose common characteristic is the "hinge factor", unexpected turning points that were decisive in changing the course of history. And it would be the crossed paths of two exceptional persons centuries ago that changed the landscape of Eastern Bohemia: First was Count Franz Anton von Sporck (František Antonín hrabě Špork, 1662–1738), whose father's military triumphs led to their great wealth; the other was Matthias Bernhard Braun (1684–1730), the son of an impoverished aristocratic Tyrolean family who was already known as a sculpture prodigy. Count Sporck became Braun's sponsor, brought him to Bohemia and showered him with commissions for his ambitious Bad Kukus (Kuks) project, which he was able to undertake, and underwrite, thanks to the wealth of money and land he inherited from his father.

Avenue to the Hospital, Kukus (Kuks)

Count Sporck, Peter J. Brandl, Kukus (Kuks)

I remember the heroes of my schoolmates in 1950s Vienna: race driver Stirling Moss, maybe Albert Einstein. Yet I never knew anyone who shared the object of my admiration or even knew his name: Imperial Count Franz Anton von Sporck. I wasn't interested in recruiting admirers; I left the count where I discovered him—our library and in the stories my father told me. Our interest was directed at two Sporcks: mine towards the son, Franz Anton junior; my father's towards the brilliant cavalry general. In 1664, the senior Sporck had helped to rout the Turks, thwarting their attack on the Empire, in a battle 150 kilometers (93 miles) from Vienna. Sporck, from a Westphalian farmer's family, ennobled for his achievements and known throughout Europe as the most skilled light rider, was the

supreme cavalry commander of the multi-ethnic Habsburg army led by Raimondo Count Montecuccoli. Sporck was rewarded by the emperor for his important military successes with estates in Bohemia, thus becoming one of the richest landowners in that region. The supranational nature of the Habsburg Empire was familiar to every Austrian military officer and child. My own father was the very embodiment of this characteristic: born in the Austrian navy port of Pola in Istria, he was the son of a German-Bohemian naval officer and a Bavarian-Austrian school teacher.

I often leafed through Gustav Pazaurek's large, illustrated book *Franz Anton, Reichsgraf von Sporck: ein Mäcen der Barockzeit und seine Lieblingsschöpfung,* *Kukus*[2]. Page after page, I studied Pazaurek's book, which impressively illustrated the younger Sporck's lofty intentions for the founding of the town of Bad Kukus, to create something unique out of nothing. I was fascinated by the elegant black-and-white photographs of larger-than-life expressive statues, the allegorical depictions of virtues and vices, grouped thematically as if in an open-air museum.

A witty and wealthy junior imperial count, Franz Anton almost realized his dream of building his own fashionable resort on his inherited land on the banks of the Elbe River, near its source in the Giant Mountains. He had almost achieved his goal before fate stepped in, and nature and man destroyed his creation. Nevertheless, as we know today, because of his ambitious, albeit failed, project, he had single-handedly made possible the creation of the Bohemian Baroque landscape. This he accomplished when he became the patron of the sculptor Matthias Bernhard Braun, whom he had met in Italy, then 'imported' him to Bohemia and showered him with artistic commissions.

For me, as an economics student in post-war Vienna, the idea of a sophisticated health and entertainment resort with a well-planned, self-contained "Gaudium" complex—comprising inns, restaurants, bathing and sports facilities, theatres, event venues, racecourses, theme nights, a zoo, board games, with a local management team as one might find today with a "destination marketing organization", with Count Sporck himself serving as the Director of Public Relations and Brand Development Manager—seemed like a glimpse into the future, as seen from the 18th century.

A few sentences and a footnote kept drawing me back to Pazaurek's book:

> *"In Kukus…around this time it was still … Sculptor Joseph* Patzelt (also "Patzak") from Altschurz, of whom we only know that he was Braun's pupil, so probably also … whose work will have been involved."*

(* Joseph was probably an uncle of Braun's pupil Georg.)

And this peculiar footnote:

> *"[Patzak] surpassed his master in decency and nobleness; nevertheless, this prominent man died in 1740 in the Kukus hospital in the greatest poverty."*

Patzak? Prominent man? Involved in the decoration of Bad Kukus? Of which you hardly know anything? From the same area as my ancestors?

While in 1900, in Pazaurek's book, the artistic record of the sculptor family Patzak was still a footnote, 60 years later it was confirmed in the standard work of the time, *Baroque Sculpture in Bohemia* by Dr. Václav Vilém Štech [3]:

> *"In Bohemian Baroque sculpture we find different stages of moving away from the central ideas embodied by Matthias Braun. The transformation can be seen in the numerous stone and carved statues that we associate with the name of the Pacák [Patzak] family, which is of great importance for the sculptural wealth of Bohemia".*

> *"Artistically, Georg (Jiří, 1664–1742) appears first and then his son Franz (František 1680–1757)… Reconstructing the development of both sculptors is not easy. … The sculptures in the Piarist Church in Leitomischl (Litomyšl), in which Georg participated as Braun's assistant, can serve as a starting point. In these works, Patzak first acted as the master's assistant and later on his own. Here, Braun's allegories had a certain angularity, and the bodies of the saints are short and heavy. The solidification of Braun's emotion is even more evident in the figures of the evangelists, where Patzak intervened independently, loosening the limbs and placing the little angels above the side entrances of the façade…. In the stone masonry work you can see the woodcarving training of the artist. Obviously, Georg and Franz learned wood carving first, although it is not certain whether from Braun himself. Both took over from Braun the types of saints, the drapery, the compositional principles and especially the evolution of the statue from the pedestal. Both Georg and his son continued Braun's principles, thought them through further and adapted them to their own themes. They expanded Braun's types with new phrases and signs."*

In 1965, in Emanuel Poche's great monograph, *Matyáš Bernard Braun* [4], Georg Patzak finally became an important secondary theme, characterized by Poche variously as *"Braun's best student"*, *"Braun's strongest competitor"*, and *"Braun's legitimate successor"*.

Experiencing Bad Kukus in 1967

During my first visit to Bad Kukus in 1967, I got to know the incomparable lecturer and guide Karel Dolézal. Already during the car ride he showed his skills as an "edu-tainer". He introduced himself as an admirer of both Sporcks and imparted many interesting details about their lives—both the courageous daredevil Johann, who had never learned to read and write, could barely put his name on paper, spent the night with his soldiers around the campfire and was a stranger to personal luxury, and his witty and well-educated son, who had developed into a patron of the arts and sciences with a wide range of interests. Dolézal recounted that General Sporck, who spoke only Low German, had told the emperor that he would not pay the usual fee for the title of count conferred on him; because "he does not buy a gift count and he does not need a paid one". As a result, Leopold I waived the usual payment.

His son, Franz Anton von Sporck (František Antonín hrabě Špork), who was brought up multilingually, began a long educational journey, a "Grand Tour", through Europe at the age of 18 and, despite occasional reservations due to his father's modest origins, had found a warm reception wherever he went. The bold deeds of the old cavalry general had engendered the respect of militaries all over the continent, since he was victorious against the aggression of a non-European power. The seriousness with which Franz Anton used his two years of travel cemented my high opinion of him: in Paris and Rome he became a confident art connoisseur and matured into an impressive personality, with masterful rhetoric and a great understanding of fine arts, architecture, music, theatre and poetry. Impressed with the traditions of *par force* hunting, he also founded the Order of St. Hubert, which still renders outstanding services to Kukus even today.

While some texts comment on his perfectionism, (which may have sprung from feelings of inferiority), his aggressiveness, and penchant for troublemaking, Dolézal and I simply admired the Count's creativity, his high intelligence, spirit of enterprise and his drive to implement his ideas, without which this very special Bohemian Baroque landscape and Bad Kukus, with its collection of artistic works, would not have existed.

Thanks to Sporck's eccentric character and the immense fortune of his warhorse father, a unique combination of architecture, sculpture, painting and nature had been created into a composed ensemble, whose *genius loci*, however, had to take many low blows from both humans and Mother Nature, from which it never recovered. Destroyed by floods in 1740, and ruined further by wrecking balls in the 20th century, one can only imagine the theatricality of the scenery: on one bank of the Elbe River the Baroque joie de vivre of the spa and "entertainment district", while the opposite river bank was dominated by healing, piety and a focus on the afterlife with its sombre, stately church and hospital on the hill. The Baroque soul, my guide mused, oscillated between the search for worldly pleasures on the one hand, and on the other a spiritual asceticism rejecting the life's vanities amid the omnipresence of death.

Sporck and his Artists: On the Same Wavelength, with Mutual Respect—and Georg Patzak on the List

Braun was by no means the only artist who had been hired to accomplish the tasks associated with the founding and development of Kukus. Sporck had won over the best sculptors and painters in Bohemia for his plans and made them respected partners in an atmosphere of teamwork between client and artist—although the term "artist" did not correspond to today's: sculptors were considered craftsmen who were often still mere serfs. Until 1782, when serfdom was abolished by Emperor Joseph II, they were bought and sold together with the manor, obliged to perform compulsory service, were not allowed to move away from the lands of the estate, were subject to the jurisdiction of the lord of the manor, including requiring his permission to marry. According to Dolézal, Sporck had nothing to complain about in principle about this social construct. But, deeply hurt by the dismissive attitude of the Bohemian nobility, who saw him as

Figure of Religion.
Matthias B. Braun.
Kukus (Kuks)

a parvenu, he created his own world on his estates, populating it with his own contacts as he saw fit. Being an aristocrat, Braun had been granted Prague citizenship at an early age, while others, such as his assistant and pupil Georg Patzak, had to fight for an exemption and a marriage license or did not receive it at all. Eventually, Patzak was released from serfdom by the Jesuits, who were owners of the estate to which he was indebted, thanks to a cleverly worded petition. Shortly thereafter, he opened his own studio as a free citizen.

There They were—The Statues from Pazaurek's Book!

Being in the presence of my old acquaintances from the pages of Pazaurek's book, the figures now battered by centuries of weather and neglect, was a powerful experience ... tangible, dignified, unforgettable. In 1967, the originals were still in the open, but as of 1984 are now protected in the Lapidarium in Kukus, and have been replaced on the original sites by copies.

Baroque Statues Tell a "Story in Stone",

Karel Doléžal was in his element: there was really no better way to explain the essence of Baroque sculpture than with his description of the statue "Allegory of Religion", based on Emanuel Poche's monograph *Matyáš Bernard Braun, sochař českého baroka a jeho dílna*:

On August 19, 1717, the Holy Trinity Church, the central building of the hospital of Kukus, was consecrated by the Bishop of Königgrätz (Hradec Králové). As early as 1712 to 1715, Matthias Braun had decorated the stone parapet of the semicircular platform in front of the church with allegorical statues of the eight Beatitudes, the execution of which, however, he entrusted to students. Only the very complex statue of religion, created around 1718, which stands freely in the middle of the platform in front of the entrance to the Sporck family crypt, is sculpted by Braun himself.

As in a *tableau vivant*, the artwork depicts a scene conceived by Sporck's poetic imagination: "Religion", represented by a young, winged woman, her right hand resting on the cross, a Bible in her left hand, her left foot on the globe she dominates and her right foot on a skeleton, the symbol of death. An eagle perched on her wing announces her triumph over death. She holds out to the viewer the Holy Scriptures, on which the first and last letters of the Greek alphabet are engraved, which, according to ancient ideas, represent the keys of the universe: Alpha and Omega, the signs of the comprehensive totality of God, and especially of Christ, as the first and last. While until the Baroque period—which began in Italy and found Europe's sculptural guiding star in Giovanni Lorenzo Bernini (1598–1680)—the goal of a sculptural work was usually an often-idealized representation of a person, Baroque sculpture was intended to depict feelings, thoughts, moods, embody a spiritual and physical liveliness, proclaim ideas. The demand for carvings of altars and other church furnishings increased so quickly, due to the surge of religious fervor, that new studios were created, yet they still could hardly keep up with the work. Statues of saints erected on streets and village squares, fountain figures, roof gable figures and, last but not least, tomb sculptures: everything was needed.

A client like Sporck, who suggested not only the themes of the statues but often also the details of the design, usually also packed a personal message or self-portrayal into his compositions: about his religiosity or charity, about a philosophical statement and about representation. Braun's achievement was to give shape to Sporck's ideas and to draw a stone figure with fluttering robes and expressive positions as an instruction sketch for his journeymen, apprentices and stone masons. Braun himself, weakened by a lung disease, rarely worked with a hammer and chisel, but ran the largest artistic production company in the country as its creative director and instructor. The sculptural work was so physically demanding that the orders were carried out by workshop assistants according to the master's templates or clay models—often very independently, depending on skills and time pressure. First, they drew the design on the front of a block of stone the size of the total volume of the statue, then sketched the depth on the flank, which was an enormous challenge to the spatial imagination, given the complexity of Braun's designs. Finally, they began to work the sandstone with a pointed hammer and tooth chisel, usually unprotected from stone dust.

Virtues v. Vices? One is the Crowd Favorite of the Bohemian Baroque

The series of representations of vices and virtues were among the highlights of Braun's workshop. The virtues include hope, love, patience, generosity. But to quote Wilhelm Busch, "Nobody is really in the mood for virtue…." The visitors near us marveled at the dramatic depictions of vices, such as avarice, gluttony, unchastity, envy, and amused themselves with associations with the larger-than-life allegorical figures, which were intended to exhort the viewer to follow the noble commandments and avoid evil, using a pictorial language understood by educated people of the 18th century.

Virtue of Justice, Matthias B. Braun, Kukus (Kuks)

In addition to these two dozen statues and eight statues representing the Beatitudes, there were several other individual orders. Clearly, Count Sporck must have been impressed by how the 35-year-old Braun managed this enormous volume of orders: first the designs, Braun's domain, which he drew

assisted by the ingenuity of the congenial client, who was about ten years older. The two strictly adhered to Cesare Ripa's *Iconography for the Representation of Virtues and Vices*, which contained precise instructions for the personification of the most diverse abstract concepts. Based on this, Braun modeled 24 female figures as clay figures, pulling out all the stops of theatricality, especially in the illustration of vices, from expressive physiognomies to dramatic exaggerations to hearty symbols: between 1718 and 1719, one of the most spectacular creations of the Baroque period was created in Braun's studio.

Art historian Gert Schiff describes Braun's form in the virtues and vices in Kukus as a "mannerist exaggeration of Bernini's form, stripped of its spiritual content."[5] Bernini created the passionate emotion, the abandonment of the cubic unity of the figure, the life of the wind-blown robes or those dissolved in whirlpools of folds. The unstable posture motifs, the precious and overloaded costume types, and finally the sculptor's playful and ironic attitude to the moral content of his allegories are manneristic.

Braun has nothing to gain from Bernini's ecstatic religiosity. Instead, he has exceptional physiognomic accuracy, proof of a thorough knowledge of human nature; his humor is equally focused on the gruesome and macabre (e.g. greed, envy, despair) and mockery (gluttony, lust). In the graceful figures such as pride and frivolity on the one hand, prudence and justice on the other, the contrast between vice and virtue is hardly noticeable. Thus, the sculptor's way of thinking triumphs over the strictly educational intention of his client.

Patzak's Involvement in the Decoration of Bad Kukus

"The clearest characteristic of Patzak's collaboration on nine statues in Kukus is the idiosyncratic design of the drapery of these figures" (Emanuel Poche and Ivo Kořán, 2003)

Already in his book, Pazaurek writes about Patzaks' collaboration in the creation of the statues for Kukus and mentions a remark by Sporck about a meeting, in which he regretfully noted that of all the artists assembled, a bilingual conversation was only possible with Patzak. Not a single other artist would have understood Czech.

At this time, Braun's studio had half a dozen experienced production teams with different skills, who worked as they saw fit and were only periodically checked by Braun. However, since the differences in the statues delivered to Bad Kukus were recognizable even to laymen, experts had tried early on to divide the statues into groups based on characteristic features that corresponded to individual production teams. The sculptor who increasingly took responsibility for commissions to Braun's workshop and acted on behalf of the ailing master, had his own business and finally became Braun's successor, was Georg F. Patzak, perhaps also Josef Patzak.

Several results of style comparisons are juxtaposed today. The arguments of Emanuel Poche and his pupil and successor, Ivo Kořán, which are published in the award-winning German edition of the monograph *Matthias Bernhard Braun*, (in German translation; 2003) [4], ascribe a very high proportion of their production to Georg Patzak. According to the authors, "The clearest proof … of Patzak's cooperation is …the idiosyncratic design of these figures."

"Today we know that already towards the end of the second decade of the 18th century, when the Kukus allegories were created, Patzak was an independent sculptor in Politschka (Polička), from where he moved to Leitomischl in 1719. Despite this contradiction between established fact and traditional account, the claims about Patzak's collaboration with Braun in Kukus do not necessarily have to have sprung from fantasy, because his stay in Politschka does not rule out such a possibility. And all the more so because the stylistic peculiarities and characteristics of certain figures of virtues and vices, which coincide with Patzak's later own work, especially with the sculptures of the statue groups in Politschka and Schatzlar (Žacléř), support the traditional attribution regarding Patzak's involvement in the sculptural decoration of Kukus. The statue's expressive physiognomy is particularly well used in the characters of the figures, (especially in gluttony), whose faces fully correspond to the realistic conception of the faces of the old women as we know them from Patzak's own statues. The clearest feature of the handling of the stone and that is proof of Patzak's cooperation—I am concerned whether this has not been blurred by the unprofessional restoration—is the idiosyncratic design of the drapery of these figures. In contrast to the dynamic grandeur and expressive language of the garment in Braun's previous works, this drapery is concrete, it respects the shape, the posture and the position of the limbs, it adheres to the surface of the body, the shallow folds tend to flow down along the body and envelop limbs as well as bodies with wavy, sensitively fluttering hems and flat curved strokes and folds. Especially on the abdomen of the figures, this design is characteristic of Patzak's later statues. At the same time, the outlines of the curvatures and folds are sharp; they were created by the wide use of the chisel, which gives the drapery a certain stiffness and a decidedly carved angularity. Viewed from a distance, we have a cascade of levels that intersect and overlap once, only to differentiate between light and shadow in soft contrasts. Thus, with no less persuasive power, the illusion of life is created, as it is created by Braun's usual, highly applied drapery, which can be seen in the allegory of faith and love."

Regarding Patzak's stylistic features, the authors add: "The stylistic idiosyncrasies and characteristics of certain figures that support Patzak's involvement in the sculptural decoration of Kukus … are three figures from the series of virtues and six from the series of vices." Karel Dolezal concluded in his analysis that:

Virtue of Chastity,
Matthias B. Braun and
Georg F. Patzak, Kukus (Kuks)

The Iconography of the Figures

Hardly any other work has influenced the allegorical pictorial worlds of the early modern period and especially Baroque art more than Cesare Ripa's *Iconologia*, which has been widely used since its first edition in 1593. His consistent personification of abstract concepts has left countless traces in paintings, frescoes and architecture. Each term in his book corresponds to a picture with a description of the allegorical figure, the type and color of its clothing, as well as evidence from the Bible and ancient literature. Sporck and Braun, and thus also Patzak, strictly adhered to Ripa's specifications, as in these nine statues that show a high proportion of Georg Patzak's artistic influence.

Excerpts from the *Explanations of the Cycle of Virtues and Vices* by Gert Schiff [7] offer details of the figures' characteristic elements.

Chastity

In every detail, chastity was formed according to the precepts of Ripa's *Iconologia*. The robe must have been white. The face is veiled, because, as St. Gregory the Great points out in his *Moralia*, it befits the chaste to keep their eyes, these nimble seducers, veiled. The right hand holds a scepter as a symbol of self-control. The left hand is about to take a pair of pigeons from the pedestal, which bears a relief of Joseph fleeing from Potiphar's seductive wife. According to Egyptian tradition, the pigeons are considered a symbol of chastity, because once the male has lost his companion, he never mates again. Although she is still leaning against the pedestal, the figure seems to be on the move: the reception of the pigeons, the groping foot in front of it, already express the desire to continue being here. In fact, Ripa demands that chastity be represented "in atto di caminare"(i.e. 'ready to walk'); it must not merely rest; since idleness is the beginning of all vices.

Sincerity

Sincerity is dressed in a garment that was originally golden, in order to illustrate at a glance the authenticity, purity and great value of this virtue. On the right, under her garment, she hides a pair of white doves that embody her purity and harmlessness; with her left hand, as a sign that she does not hide anything, she holds out her heart to the world.

"Patzak's artistic greatness is evident in much more than just the drapery."
He was impressed by the richness of detail in the draperies, but this alone was too restrictive, too "mechanistic" and "reductionistic", as he put it and as I understood him. "Drapery is all well and good, but please look at the artistic expression of his characters! It would be a shame to reduce Patzak's art to drapery! In Kukus, too, Patzak's artistic genius is not only recognizable by the type of drapery. Look at the figures in strong movement, often *contrapposto* instead of a frontal position, rich robes in flowing abundance, finely-modelled hands with strong expressiveness, graceful heads with hauntingly animated features, small mouths and fine, long, straight noses." It seems as if the scholarly, meticulous search for the contemporaneous evidence, for documents and records, which prove Patzak's role in the design of Bad Kukus, would still offer a lot of material for historians, since one already has a supposedly scientific opinion, based on stylistic comparisons.

Industry

In her raised hand, the female figure holds an iron cone with yarn. The beehive symbolizes hard work, the hourglass indicated that diligent people value their time. The rooster reminds us that the diligent get up early in the morning.

Envy

The iconologist thinks of envy as an old, ugly, pale, withered woman with a mischievous look, in a neglected, rust-colored robe; her hair full of snakes and eating her own heart. She is old because she has long been at odds with virtue. The snakes symbolize poisonous thoughts; when she consumes her own heart, it shows the way envy punishes itself. Attached to the figure is a half-starved, snarling dog; a good example of how far-fetched some of these allegories are. Ripa says that the dog is considered to be an envious animal that hoards things for itself.

Lust

In the design of the figure for this vice, Braun differs from Ripa. When he lets them trample wealth and learning, one thinks one feels the guidance of Count Sporck; everything else, however, belongs to the realm of the comical, and should therefore be assumed to be Braun's idea. As with Ripa, the figure gazes at the mirror. Instead of the usual ermine, however, Braun makes her companion a monkey, an older symbol of lewdness. The juxtaposition of the woman and the monkey creates a visual punchline: in the flat scratch relief, the mirror reflects the features of the monkey, which is also staring at the mirror; expecting to enjoy the sight of her own beauty in the mirror, the woman is instead confronted with the apeish grin of her own intemperance.

Gluttony

At no point is Braun's ironic attitude to the moral allegories assigned to him more evident than in this figure. Everywhere in the art of the Renaissance as well as in the Baroque, the cult of Bacchus is the epitome of the "high life". Here, Braun places a wreath of Bacchic vines around a pig, the embodiment of gluttony.

Sloth

Braun does not condemn the figure of inertia, but sympathetically depicts how she dozes off obliviously, while leaning on the neck and rump of her donkey. According to Ripa's misguided erudition,

Vices of Envy, Matthias B. Braun and Georg F. Patzak, Kukus (Kuks)

the donkey served the Egyptians as a symbol of a low spirit that is far removed from all sacred and religious objects, so this is the true curse of sloth. But here the donkey is nothing more than the patient and reliable companion who will save his mistress from falling if she should slip further from mere dozing into sleep.

Despair

Suicidal despair, which the sculptor depicts not only as sinful but also foolish, should, according to Ripa, still hold a cypress branch in his left hand, because just as such a man's hand does not grow back when cut off, the man who surrenders to despair kills every speck of virtue or noble deeds within himself. Braun, on the other hand, makes him clearly reach urgently for the rope.

Guile

The mask is an obvious symbol of malice and fraud. The piercing eyes and full lips are there to beguile and betray. Seen in full figure, its duplicity becomes apparent; the robe is distinctly divided in two along the middle of the body. Of course, the sly fox is her companion. In her right hand is a squid; just as the squid hides from the fisherman in its black ink, so the deceitful person exists in a dark web of lies.

It seems that this marked the end of Patzak's collaboration with Braun's studio for the sculptural design of Bad Kukus. Between 1718 and 1719, he played a decisive role in one of the most witty and imaginative creations of the Baroque era. Emanuel Poche commented on Patzak's final departure from Braun's workshop, "With Patzak's departure, Braun's workshop lost a skillful and artistically gifted journeyman, and perhaps it was precisely his departure that caused the unsatisfactory quality of certain sculptures in the church of Leitomischl that were left unfinished." And we are reminded that Poche considered Patzak to be "*Braun's best student*", "*Braun's strongest competitor*", and "*Braun's legitimate successor*".

1 Durschmied Karl: Hinge-Faktor. Wie Zufälle Weltgeschichte schreiben. , Böhlau, Wien 1998
2 Pazaurek, Gustav: Franz Anton, Reichsgraf von Sporck: ein Mäcen der Barockzeit und seine Lieblingsschöpfung Kukus, Leipzig 1901.
3 Štech,Václav V.: Die Barockskulptur in Böhmen, Artia Verlag, Prag 1959.
4 Poche Eduard: Matthias Bernhard Braun, Studien Verlag, Innsbruck 2003.
5 Schiff, Gert: Erläuterungen zum Zyklus der Tugenden und Laster, DU Verlag, Zürich 1963.

Additionally

Interview from 1973 in World Travel Digest Magazine with Dr. Heinz Patzak, North America Chairman European Travel Commission (ETC)
Tilden, Freeman: Interpreting our Heritage, 3rd edition, N. Carolina Press 2008.
Bibliography

St. Mary Immaculata,
Georg F. Patzak,
Schurz (Žireč)

I.3
The Religious Source of Power of the Stilo Moderno
(Heinz Patzak)

The "stilo moderno", which was given the name "Baroque" much later and nowadays refers to an art movement as well as to a period of history, not only transformed our landscape, churches, palaces, and culture, but also left traces in the European mindset. The spiritual and secular leaders, the abbeys and corporations all over Europe made use of the Baroque style to impress, instruct, influence and entertain people. It was not the result of a branding effort—"Power enabled by Art"—but rather, arose organically.

"You need chaos in your soul to give birth to a dancing star."
F. Nietzsche

The Baroque—a chronology

From 1515:
The "secchezza" [dryness] of the Renaissance begins to bore artists. Italy, then the undisputed center of European art, is producing hardly any new work in the Renaissance style. A new image of man emerges, with a strong emphasis on the individual. A new style is also emerging, deep within the artists themselves. In their hands, the formal development of a style has its own life and logic. It is conditioned by the artist's material, his inventiveness and his passion to explore his own artistic potential to the fullest. The financial support and artistic latitude of church commissions allow for the constant regeneration of the creative heart of art. Only here could the artist bring to fruition his irrepressible longing for greatness and his passion for transcending the boundaries of strict form, and lose himself in the boundless space of possibility.
Working in the churches, the sculptor develops his sense of proportion, the painter his sense of movement, light and shadow, as well as the tricks of perspective. The emergence of an art style usually fits in with the societal milieu in which the artist lives and works; indeed they reinforce each other. Thus, the Baroque became the unmistakable trademark of the successful Catholic reform, on the basis of which the primacy of the Catholic Church was reestablished with piety made beautifully visual.

From 1517:
The administrator of the treasury in the Escorial enters a new addition to the inventory, an uneven crooked pearl, and notes it with a negative term from the jeweler's vocabulary, *barroco*. It's also been theorized that the word "Baroque" is a derivation of the Italian word "parrucca" (wig), with "wig style" being an insult wielded by the often vituperative advocates of classical aesthetics, who also sometimes saw an additional association with the "barbaric", proven by the first syllable of the term. Additionally, incipient nationalism plays a role: for a long time, a considerable part of the French art world turned up its nose at the Italian Baroque, while at the same time, both Paris and Rome invoke Tacitus and his negative view of the Germanic tribes to make their negative judgement of the Baroque in Germany. In Germany itself, the territorial fragmentation is compounded by an aggressive anti-Catholicism, ensuring that contempt for the Baroque lasts for a long time.
The devaluation carried out by some of the leading French academies in Europe at the time, with a nationalist political undertone, goes so far as to claim that the Baroque was merely a degenerate art that had emerged in Italy and that its artists were mentally ill. The enemies of the Baroque were concerned with a central focus of the Enlightenment: to return to the ancient model in art and, thus, to reason and the imitation of nature. In order to achieve this ideal, one needs the antithesis of the Baroque, an anti-classicism that makes classicism shine all the more brightly.

And they went even further: in some razor-sharp French art critiques, "baroque" and "gothic" were used interchangeably for "grotesque", "bizarre", because for some authors of this period, the Gothic was also an anti-classical style that did not correspond to what they considered the valid norm. In addition, the name, with its reference to the Goths, who were considered Eastern European hordes, offers the Puritan "classics" targets for attack: for them, Baroque remained ugly and Gothic barbaric. It took more than a century for France to accept the Gothic as its national style and to reevaluate and appreciate the Baroque for its powerful painterly effect. To this day, the expression, which is phonetically easy to use in all languages, remains ambivalent, forever associated with pejorative terms of taste for the anti-classical, irregular, exaggerated, fashionably bizarre, but at the same time evocative of some of the greatest achievements in art and music.

From 1520:
As a reaction to certain grievances about the Roman Catholic Church, there arose an ecclesiastical renewal movement, the Reformation, initiated in German-speaking countries and spread quickly via the critical writings of the Augustinian monk Martin Luther.

From 1522:
As a result of the Reformation's rejection of all forms of veneration of Mary or saints, iconoclasm increasingly removed all portraits and sculptures from churches, and frescoes were whitewashed or chiseled out of the walls. The baptismal font and a communion table with an open Bible replaced the altar, which was banished in many Protestant churches.

From 1540:
The Roman Catholic Church reacts, and the Counter-Reformation begins. The tranquility of the Renaissance is thus broken; everything is in motion. For the Pope, the Turkish wars and the need to fortify Rome militarily are not so much a threat as the "invasion" of a Puritan spirit alien to him. So he "fortifies" Rome, as it were, by decorating the city with Catholic images and purposefully dedicating the arts to the Church. The age of the Counter-Reformation is passionate, full of fear and ecstasy. Buoyed by new prosperity, this energy spills over into the arts, which become the perfect propaganda tool. With the help of the artists, it was thought that the goal of stopping the Lutheran successes could be achieved.

1545–1563: The Council of Trent and the Catholic Reformation
The formal safeguarding, which was no less important for the coming world presence of Baroque art, took place in the Alps, at the Council of Trent. In the course of the Catholic reform, important decisions were made there on the construction of churches, including the introduction of the high altar. The Protestant practice of removing pictorial decorations from their churches is rejected with theological logic: "The invisible God is visible through the incarnation and can therefore be represented by the Roman Catholic Church." Martin Luther himself is not an iconoclast for practical reasons. Since very few people can read the Bible, he sees the illustrations as a way to bring people closer to the biblical stories.

From 1550:
The Pope approves the constitution of the Jesuit Society, Societas Jesu, S.J., founded a few years earlier in Paris. Since a desired missionary activity in Palestine does not materialize, they go to Rome and make themselves available to the Pope—"for the defense and spread of the faith". They were building a modern Christian education system, to replace a mediocre one, to raise the educational level of the general population and train future leaders. The practical and modern character of the new society, which played a major role in the Counter-Reformation, ensured sympathy for contemporary art. The fact that the community needs churches brings its members into direct contact with the world of art, and the churches built and decorated in the new way quickly lead to the term "Jesuit" being equated with Baroque art.
It is tempting to want to find the spirit of its age in each new style. It is true that in the Gothic period one finds evidence of the prevailing feudalism and

St. Charles Borromeo with Crucifix, Georg F. Patzak, Politschka (Polička)

Archangel Raphael, Georg F. Patzak, Lusche (Luže)

scholasticism of the Middle Ages, and if one thinks of the art of the Renaissance, one is drawn into the atmosphere of a diligent luxurious silence, into a tranquility to which one indulges in seclusion or in exquisite company. In the Baroque, on the other hand, the analogies are obvious. The Baroque century brings turmoil and controversy. Revolution and reformation are on the rise. Representatives of the Church sat in council or stood up to fiercely arguing crowds, gesticulating in pulpits or ministering abroad in leprosy wards and on galleys.

From 1600:
Baroque—timeless emotions expressed in controlled commissioned art to achieve religious goals? Novel realistic and rousing depictions of ruler representation? The age of the Baroque is also the age of reason, and the search for the mathematically logical handwriting of God in nature. Artists have to comply with established "decorum" and strict rules of artistic expression. In the case of larger building complexes, such as a church or a palace, the artists are organized into groups working on the project, and must strictly adhere to the arrangement of the architect and the author of the iconographic program. The position of the many sculptors and carvers was considered to be lower than that of the painters. They are craftsmen with relatively high incomes.

There are guilds, workshops, artists' colonies, artists who are employees of state organizations or patrons, as well as serfs and religious artists. Through the ancient tradition of itineration, artists from other parts of Europe travel to the most remote areas of the province to practice their craft. The first art academies are established. The themes are deliberately chosen to display the Catholic faith and those principles that are the particular objects of the Reformation attacks: the Eucharist, the angels, the devotion to the Blessed Virgin Mary, the cult of saints, the sacraments, the effectiveness of good works and the authority of Rome. In the early years of the Jesuit Order, when destruction and persecution raged in Germany, Scandinavia and especially in England, the Jesuit novices from these countries were so confronted with scenes of martyrdom and death that the nerves of the newcomers were on edge in the face of the deadly realities that awaited them.

El Greco—Rubens—Bernini

The leading figures who make Baroque art quintessentially European are the great names of the seventeenth century: El Greco in Toledo, who creates the earliest Baroque paintings; Rubens in Flanders, the technical master of European painting; and Bernini in Rome, architect, sculptor and painter whose activities sum up the entire Baroque spirit. These three men find their intellectual basis in Jesuit aesthetics and maintain close personal ties with the Order. It is characteristic of Baroque art, which is so expressive, that it pushes the boundaries of the arts. That is why the Jesuits are so interested in theatrical performances. They used many elements that we consider modern: lighting effects, the revolving stage, the participation of the audience in what is happening on stage, as typified in the Passion Play.

From c. 1780:

At the end of the 18th century, resistance began to stir, and the opinion spread that the expressiveness of the Baroque was exaggerated, disingenuous and theatrical, or at least seemed so. The obvious answer lies in pointing out the purpose of the Catholic Reformation and the circumstances and place where the style originated.

In the 19th century, everything is very different from that found in a Cistercian community, and the task of communication—one of the functions of art in the church—must of necessity take on a special form when it is addressed to people outside the monastery walls. In contrast to ascetic ideals, the opulence of the Baroque appears to be wild and worldly—as is its energy and appeal to emotions. It stands out strongly from the brooding solemnity of Romanesque architecture, as it seems impetuous and theatrical. But if one approaches the Baroque in its contemporary spirit and free from conventional opinion, these superficial opposites lose their power. There is a new mysticism, a new force that does not necessarily exude a monastic spirit and does not separate itself from the world, but also incorporates secular elements thus enabling the Church to achieve the same final result.

While historians can live happily with the naming of the epochs before and after the Baroque as Renaissance or Classicism, it would not be the Baroque if it did not inspire heated conference debates and brilliant specialist articles on how to describe the epoch between 1500 and 1770.

It was to be expected that a negatively branded term such as "absolutism" would be out of the question. It, too, was a product of the upheavals of the religious wars, and a monarchical form of government that granted the ruler—as it turned out, often just on paper—unlimited and undivided state power. In the history of art history, the Baroque had a hard time establishing itself as a stylistic term, but today a number of historians advocate the epochal designation "Baroque" and "Enlightenment". This would be congruent with the trend in historical scholarship to no longer orient the concepts of epochs to great politics, but to social and cultural history. Furthermore, in contrast to absolutism, the Baroque spread over most of Europe as a phenomenon in the history of art, music and literature and was organic in origin. From the obscure word for a second-rate pearl to the most reviled term of the classic academies to the celebrated designation for one of the most successful epochs of mankind ….

"*La vérité vaut bien qu'on passe quelques années sans la trouver.** (Jules Renard, 1864–1910)

**The truth is well worth spending a few years without finding it.*"

Angel of Death, Matthias B. Braun, Kukus (Kuks)

I. 4
Born—Being—Perishing—Being—Kukus is Living!
(Mag. Sweerts-Sporck)

Count Sporck is as well known in the Czech Republic as General Albrecht von Wallenstein, commander of the Holy Roman Emperor's armies during the Thirty Years' War. Stephan Sweerts-Sporck, a descendant of the Count, lives in Kukus, the cultural heritage of the Sporcks. He tries to track down this high level of awareness. It has to be more than just the outwardly visible buildings and figures. Maybe it's a mysticism that Kukus radiates? Count Sporck, for all his human weaknesses, had ultimately lived for and loved his fellow human beings and the Lord God. To portray him as an Antichrist because of the occasional dispute with the neighboring Schurzer Jesuits is certainly wrong. Today, Kukus thrives with splendour and a spirit of joy and celebration as well as the memories of its beginning, made visible in the Baroque statues: "Remember, oh man, where you come from and where you are going." Likewise, the gardens in Kukus demonstrate their perennial cycles of rebirth.

I.5
Joy of Living—Born Out of the Ashes of War
(Gerhard Honal)

It's hard to imagine, but the terrible Thirty Years' War from 1618 to 1648, both a religious conflict and a power struggle between the ruling houses of Europe, brought about joy in the world, expressed in the music, literature, visual and performing arts of the Baroque period. Because with this, the fear of death and the longing for redemption could be overcome sooner than with further violence. About a third of the inhabitants of Bohemia had lost their lives. The historian Gerhard Honal describes the fateful development from 1618 onwards. From the ashes of this war, as an expression of joie de vivre, emerges the flowering of the Baroque.

I.6 The Church in Europe is Reformed Three Times

(Werner H. Honal)

Jan Hus, a Czech Catholic priest, preaches the reform of the Church a century before Martin Luther. In his 1420 *Four Articles of Prague*, he demanded, among other things, the Lord's Supper be offered in both forms (host and wine), and the use of the national language instead of Latin in church proclamations. In order to enforce the reform, the murderous "Hussite Wars" raged until 1436, which left devastating traces in the Trautenau district, for example. The Patzaks may well have belonged to the German settlers who were recruited from Silesia at the time to replace workers killed in the conflict.

In 1517, Martin Luther presented 95 theses on the reform of the Catholic Church, which it opposed and so lost two-thirds of the Czechs, who became Lutheran. Only the third reform, the "Catholic Reform" painstakingly developed at the Council of Trent from 1545 to 1563 in response to Jan Hus and Martin Luther, corrected some serious flaws in the Catholic Church.

St. Adalbert, Franz Patzak, Leitomischl (Litomyšl)

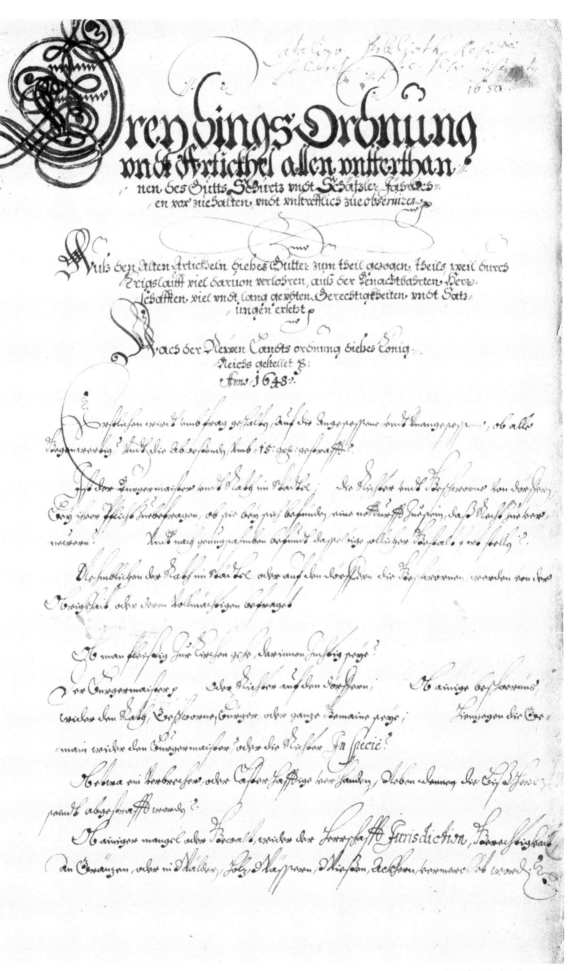

Dreydings Ordnung
vnd Artickhel allen vntterthanen des Gutts Schurtz vnd Schatzler Jahres en vor niedzuhalten vnd vntrefflich zue observiren

Auß den Alten Artickhein hiehes Gutter zum theil gezogen, theils weil durch Kriegslauff viel darvon verlohren, auß der Benachbahrten Herrschafften viel vnd lang geübten Gerechtigkheiten vnd Satzungen ersetzt

Auch der Newen Lannds ordnung diehes König Reichs gestellet B:
Anno 1648:

Drittliehen wird vmb frag gestellt, Auch die angesessene vnd Innungsposen, ob alle Zugemessen? Auch die debeschuldt vmb 15 gr: geforderst?

Ob der Burgermaister vnd Rath in Vortel, die Richter vnd Beschworne von der Herrschafft ihres Fleiß vnderfragen, ob sie bey sich befinden, eine notturfft Person, das Raths hirhervon machen? Vnd nach gennugsammen erkundt dahroüber völliger Beschlueß erfolgt?

Nochmallichen der Rath in Vortel, oder auch vor Ihnen die Beschwornen werden von der Obrigkheit oder deren Vollmächtigen besraget.

Ob man fleissig zur Kirchen gehe, darinnen Andacht prege? Der Burgermaister oder Richter auff den Dorffern, khainige beschwärnuß wieder den Rath, Beschworne, Richter oder gantze Gemaine pregt; Hingegen die Gemain wieder den Burgermaister oder die Richter In specie?

Ob ein verbrecher oder Lasterhafftige Person stecken, Neben denen die Erisch Jaßpundt abgestrafft worden?

Khaininger mangel oder Breschl, wieder der Herrschafft Jurisdiction, Baurechtighait an Grenitzen, oder in Walden, Holtz, Wassern, Wiesen, Äckhern, vorwerer beraid?

Dreyding Order, Document, Schurz (Žireč)

St. Franz-Xaver, Josef or Georg F. Patzak, Schurz (Žireč)

I.7
The Era of the Baroque Sculptors Patzak
(W. Honal/ H. Patzak)

The Baroque sculptors Patzak were serfs attached to lands controlled by its regional rulers, so they could not move freely around the country. Serfs could not leave the manor, or even marry, without approval of the rulers, whom they were obliged to serve without compensation. We found the "Dreydingsordnung", in which the Jesuits in the Trautenau area regulated the behavior of their subjects, including the Patzaks. It vividly depicts the world in which the serfs lived at that time, which is hardly imaginable today.
The letters of Georg F. Patzak to the Jesuit rulers, which were only discovered in the Leitomischl archives by Josef Tejkl in the 1970s, show how he succeeded in being freed from this serfdom.

I.8
Carvers of the Viennese Jesuits, Master Braun's Successors
(Jan Pipek)

Until the middle of the 20th century, the sculptor Josef Patzak was considered the court sculptor of the Jesuits in Schurz and the masterful successor to Matthias Bernhard Braun. Insofar as Baroque statues could not be attributed to Georg Patzak explicitly or by signatures, Josef Patzak was considered their creator. In 1938, the art historian Emanuel Poche discovered contradictions in the life stories of Josef and Georg Patzak. His explanation was that it was customary at that time for the workshop master (Josef Patzak) to mark the works of his students (Georg Patzak) with his own name. Jan Pipek was not satisfied with this solution; he finds a surprising alternate explanation.

Mariahilf Church,
Georg F. Patzak,
Lusche (Luże)

I.9
The Source of Creativity of Georg F. Patzak
(Peter Patzak)

Peter Patzak analyzes a surviving letter written by Georg F. Patzak to the superior of the Jesuits. For them, Georg had enthusiastically designed the interior of the Mariahilf Church on the Kulm in Lusche.
Precisely because of the restrictions as a subject, the splendor of his Baroque art testifies to a deep religious conviction.

1.10
The Baroque Drama of Eastern Bohemia
(Ivo Kořán)

Prof. Ivo Kořán is the Czech art historian, still alive today, who since the late 1950s has expounded on his foremost field of interest, the connections between medieval and Baroque culture and art. In his research, he notes that especially in Eastern Bohemia there was a large group of sculptors, "like a dragon with many heads", who had outgrown the Central European conventions with their art. One reason for this could have been the workshops of Matthias Bernhard Braun and the Patzaks.

Engraving Kukus,
Michael H. Renz,
Kukus (Kuks)

I.11
The Family of Baroque Sculptors Patzak / Pacák
(Werner H. Honal)

All three Baroque sculptors from the Patzak family came from East Bohemia / Východní Čechy. This is the area south of the Giants Mountains (Krkonoše), around the district capital Königgrätz (Hradec Králové). They lived between 1640 and 1757, during the early modern period.

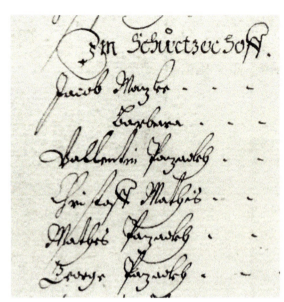

1651 Paczackh, Document, Schurz (Žireč)

The two older ones, Josef and Georg, come from the lordship of Schurz-Schatzlar, which was under the Jesuit order from 1636 to 1773. In 1636, Emperor Ferdinand II had given it to the Viennese Jesuits of St. Anna so that they could proselytize there again for the right faith after the devastating Thirty Years' War. In the "List of Faith" of 1651, (a total record of all persons living in the respective dominion older than 8 years of age, which was unique in the world at the time), the Patzak family is also listed in the soul list of subjects in the Königgrätz area (Soupis poddaných Hradecko).

However, these records did not reflect the Czech spelling "Pacák" or the German "Patzak". Such distinctions did not play a role at the time. For example, the capital of the Kingdom of Čechy was Prag, Prague and Praha, and the capital of the Margraviate of Moravia was Brünn and Brno.

The Schurzer Jesuits wrote "Paczackh" (in the picture "Am Schurzer Hof" lived, among others, see at the bottom: Mathes Paczackh and George Paczackh).
And the land register of Alt-Rognitz (Vs Žireč, kniha č. 103), kept from 1671–1783 included landowners Hans Pazackh and Georg Pazackh. A little later, however, these Paczackh families are consistently listed as Patzak in the church registers—there are no registry offices there until 1938—at baptisms, weddings and deaths. Georg Patzak lived in Schurz from 1617 to 1687 as a Schurzer Schaffer.

Paczackh, Pazackh, Patzalt, Patzak and Pacák are Czech surnames for German settlers; those recruited from Silesia to the south side of the Giant Mountains around the year 1500 probably got the name from the Czechs already living there as a nickname. The nickname may have appeared because the head of this family is responsible for the change, the "patz" (4 Kreuzer). Or he was known for his strong handshake, the "pac". Patzak was the money changer, so to speak, or, less likely, the batsman as we know him in cricket today.

A widespread theory that the name came from the German word "patzen" is wrong. The surname Patzak originated before 1600, but the word "patzen" does not appear in the German language until the 19th century.

The Baroque Sculptor Josef Patzak
Until the middle of the 20th century, all specialist encyclopedias usually listed only the Baroque sculptor Josef Patzak. Josef Patzak, who was also a painter and carver, ran a sculptor's workshop in Schurz.

The Prague art historian Emanuel Poche suspects (in his essay *K otázce činnosti sochaře Josefa Pacáka / On the question of the activities of the sculptor Josef Patzak*, Umění XI, 1938) that in the past many works by Georg Patzak, such as the well-known statue of St. Francis Xavier on the Schurzer Mühlberg,

Big Fire,
Document,
Schurz (Žireč)

were still attributed to his father, Josef, the owner of the workshop.
In 1930 Josef was named as an artist on a postcard from the high altar in the church in Swichin (Zvičina, see below).

Already in the encyclopedia *Illustrations of Bohemian and Moravian Scholars and Artists* (Pelzel 1782) Josef Patzalt / Patzak of Matthias Bernhard Braun is called "most excellent student". "He [Patzak] gave back to his master [Braun] what was honest and noble." … "Never venturing abroad, he settled down at home in his native Schurz; it is in the border mountains there, and in Silesia, where his most important works can be found." The chronicler Jaroslav Schaller mentions Josef in the Topography of the Kingdom of Bohemia (1790) in the section on Schurz and Dubenetz (15th part, pp. 65 / 66), the "famous sculptor Patzalt" who was "born here [in Schurz]". In the 4th volume of *The Kingdom of Bohemia* (1836, p.88), Johann Gottfried Sommer solves the riddle of the spelling Patzalt: "Alt-Schurz is the birthplace of the sculptor Josef Patzalt (usually called Patzak), famous in his time, who was born here towards the end of the XVII century and, after he had brought a lot of monuments of his art to this area, namely, on the lordship of Gradlitz, died in the Kukus hospital in 1740 in the greatest poverty."

Today there is great uncertainty about the personage of Josef Patzak. A devastating fire on April 1, 1825 (see picture from the local chronicle) in the former Jesuit residence in Schurz, which also affected much of the village, destroyed all the houses. In Vienna, then the capital of the German Empire, many documents of the Jesuits, who were often the patrons of the sculptors Patzak, have been lost due to rigorous clean-up work after secularization. But can the artists disappear after the destruction of the documents? Did a theory that is common today

Postcard from Switschin,
Franz Patzak,
Switschin (Zvičina)

The Baroque sculptor Georg Patzak

Georg Franz Patzak (Jirí František Pacák), was probably born around 1670 in Alt Rognitz near Trautenau (Starý Rokytník u Trutnova). Here, too, the exact dates are uncertain, as unfortunately the church register prior to 1709 has disappeared. Georg Franz Patzak is considered the greatest domestic sculptor of the dynamic Bohemian Baroque. From 1702 to 1714, he worked for the Jesuits in the pilgrimage church in Lusche, and from 1716 to 1719 he lived in Politschka, but we do not know for sure about his work from this period. He also may have worked in Kukus during this time. From 1719 until his death in 1742, he worked in Litomyšl. In 1727, he carved the statues of St. Michael and St. George (on the fountain) and St. John of Nepomuk (on the south side of the town hall) in Politschka, but his most important work there is undoubtedly the Marian obelisk (1727–1731), a very large Marian column.

Sign of Georg F. Patzak,
document,
Lusche (Luže)

Monogram of Georg F. Patzak,
Georg F. Patzak,
Dobschenitz (Dobřenice)

assume that the local pastor of Schurz simply invent Josef Patzak? If there is no evidence, there is plenty of room for hypotheses. This could also be investigated in regional land registers, contracts and in other branches of the Jesuits, e.g. in Kuttenberg (Kutná Hora), or in the Central Archives in Rome. For seventy years, the subject of "ecclesiastical Baroque art" was taboo in the Czech Republic. It did not fit in with either nationalism or Marxist communism. It was not until a layman in the field of Baroque sculpture, Josef Tejkl (1952–2009), a theatre director and head of a theatre school in Königgrätz, discovered important, hitherto neglected Jesuit documents in the Leitomischl Archives, and new impetus was given to Patzak research (1981, Umění XXIX). Mgr. Jan Bouček, now working at the National Literary Archives in Prague, attended Karls-Universität in 2015, and now for the first time, Prague will once again contribute a very commendable, comprehensive diploma thesis on the Baroque art of the Patzaks of European art history.

Marian Culumn,
Georg F. Patzak,
Schatzlar (Žacléř)

Mensis et Dies	Locus	Persona Mortua	Annus	Mensis v Dies		
1742 August 11	Leito-mischl	Georg Patzack statuarius = Bildhauer	72			

Cerificate of Death of Georg F. Patzak, Document, Moravian Trübau (Moravská Třebová)

The artist himself signed his letters (see picture), also those in Czech, with "Georg Patzak" (without Franz / František). His monogram G.P. was discovered in Lusche, and later G.F.P. in Dobschenitz.

In the church register of Moravian Trübau the entry of 11 August 1742 about the death of Georg F. Patzak indicates that he died at the age of 72 years. Since such information is often uncertain, it can be assumed that he was born around the year 1670. So, at the time of the start of work in Chlumek, he was about thirty years old. Numerous entries from this period bear witness to his "godfather" designation and his popularity in Lusche. They also identify this "godfather Jirík, carver from Chlumek" as Georg F. Patzak and son of Matthes from the village of Alt-Rognitz near Trautenau, which was part of the dominion of the Viennese Jesuits in Schurz.

Georg F. Patzak worked in the church in Chlumek as a serf of the Jesuits in Schurz, and on 22 September (or November), 1707, he married Marta Chourová, herself an employee of the Jesuits in Chlumek. The two fiancés were released from serfdom shortly before the wedding. In Lusche, the couple had two daughters and a son, Franz Heinrich, who also became a sculptor. Georg remained in Lusche until 1715, completing his work on the interior of the pilgrimage church. Then he quickly left Chlumek with his family, even before the outbreak of the plague in the autumn of 1715, and moved to Politschka, where he created a number of masterly works, especially the monumental Marian / Plague Column.

In 1721 he worked with the younger Baroque master Matthias Bernhard Braun (1684–1738) on the sculptures for the Piarist Church for the discovery of the Holy Cross in Leitomischl. In August 1719 he acquired a house from the councillors in the lower suburb of Leitomischl, where he now settled down permanently. From 1725 onwards, he designed and developed a large Marian column in Schatzlar on behalf of the Jesuit order. He returned in 1732 to decorate the Trinity Church there.

The year 1727 seems to be a particularly productive one in the work of Georg F. Patzak. In that year he carved the fountains in Politschka and completed statues of saints. In 1728, after the death of his wife Marta, he married Anna Marie David, the widow of the painter Christian Franz David. Georg F. Patzak died on 11 August 1742 in Mährisch Trübau.

The Baroque Sculptor Franz Patzak

Franz Patzak (František Pacák), was born on 29 December 1713 in Lusche, the son of Georg Franz Patzak (Jiří Pacák), and his wife Marta Chourová. He learned sculpture from his father and worked in Leitomischl, and as decreed in Georg's will, took over his father's workshop.

Aaron,
Franz Patzak,
Leitomischl (Litomyšl)

Some of his works were already in the style of the late Baroque. According to the *Biographical Encyclopedia of the Austrian Empire* (C. von Wurzbach, Part 21, 1870), he mainly created "altars, statues and Stations of the Cross—for Patzak was also a painter—in the deanery and Piarist churches in Litomyšl, as well as in the deanery church in Politschka, which was subsequently destroyed by fires and other misfortunes."

Among Franz Patzak's students was Dominik Auliczek, who later artistically managed the Nymphenburg porcelain factory and erected figures in the park of the Nymphenburg Palace. On November 24, 1750, Franz Patzak married Sofie Auliczek / Žofie Aulíčková, the older sister of Dominik Auliczek, in Politschka.

Franz Patzak died on August 17, 1757 in Leitomischl. His wife, Sofie, survived him by forty years and in 1760 gave birth to a son named Josef Franz Patzak, whose biological father, however, was not Franz, but her second husband, whom she married a month after the birth.

Neptune,
Dominik Auliczek,
Munich (München)

II.

Working Angels on the Meadow,
Georg F. Patzak, Lusche (Luže)

Pulpit,
Georg F. Patzak,
Lusche (Luže)

II. A Closer Look at Some Baroque Artworks

St. Mary, Georg F. Patzak, Lusche (Luže)

II.1
Sculptors—Wood Carvers—Gilder
(Zdenka Paukrtová)

From 1702 to 1715, Georg F. Patzak's first major commission was to decorate the interior of the pilgrimage church Mariahilf on the Kulm above Lusche. One of the most precious works there is the group of figures of the Annunciation on the dome of the Chapel of St. Mary, carved in 1705. Unusual are the figures in the pulpit with the scene on Mount Tabor, where the celestial sphere connects with the earthly one. The group of angels who skillfully and enthusiastically build in the heavenly meadow (see p. 50/51) are an effective iconographic innovation that did not exist before. Patzak's long creative period in this Mariahilfkirche enables the author and Czech art historian Zdenka Paukrtová to show the developments in Patzak's art.

II.2
The Pietà at Abtsdorf (Opatov)
(Ludmilla Kesselgruberová)

Georg F. Patzak and his son Franz Patzak not only lived in Leitomischl, they also created excellent and well-known Baroque works of art there. In the regional museum there is also a small polychrome Pietà. However, Patzak carved the large Pietà in the church of St. Anthony in the neighbouring village of Abtdorf (Opatova) in a completely different way.

Astonishingly, this high-quality carving of a Pietà has hardly been noticed in art literature so far. The art teacher PhDr. Ludmila Kesselgruberová helps us to discover the beauty of this figure. In doing so, she describes how the artist Georg F. Patzak succeeded in conveying an intense emotional mood to the viewer.

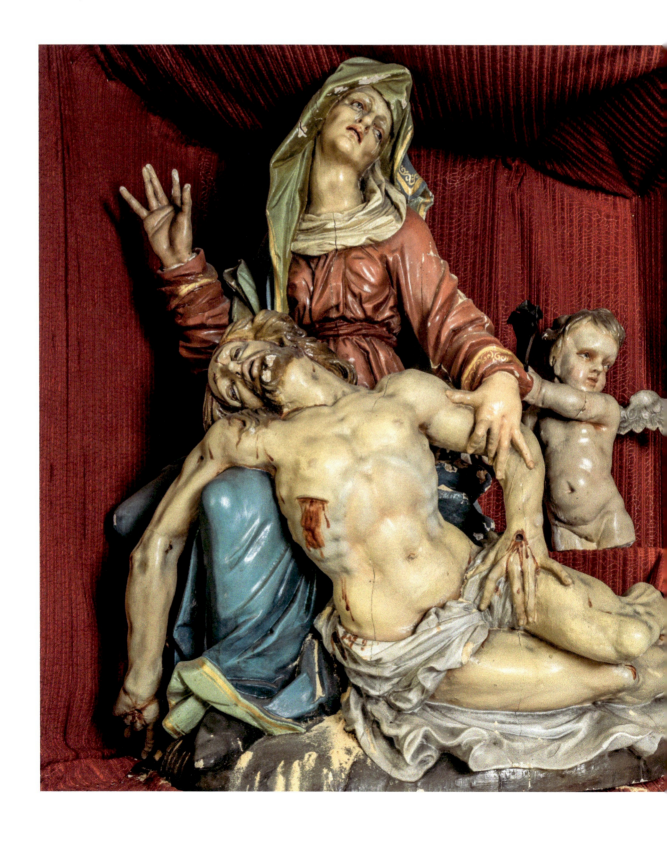

Pieta,
Georg F. Patzak,
Abtsdorf (Opatov)

Marian Obelisk,
Georg F. Patzak,
Politschka (Polička)

II.3
Politschka, the Baroque Jewel
(David Junek)

Patzak's masterpiece: the Obelisk of the Virgin Mary, the heart of one of the most beautiful squares in Central Europe[1]

Politschka (Polička)

The first three quarters of the 18th century are referred to as the "Golden Age" of Politschka, a period of economic and artistic boom in the East Bohemian city. During that time, the city underwent a significant transformation: its roads were repaved, houses got their impressive Baroque facades and the parish church was splendidly furnished. Politschka's ultimate architectural showpieces from the Baroque period are the town hall and the Marian obelisk, also known as the Marian (or plague) column. Today, only traces of that Baroque splendour remain, those monuments speak to it, as do the sights described below.

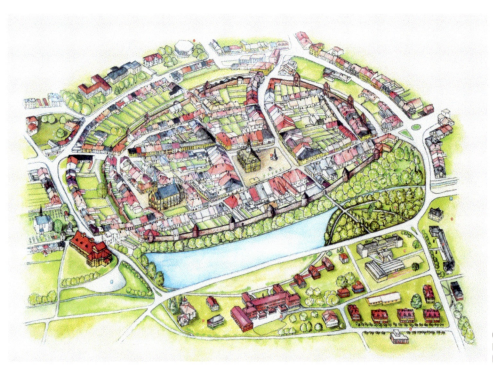

Old Town, Document, Politschka (Polička)

Baroque Buildings

In 1265, the Bohemian king Přemysl Ottokar II made Policz—the royal town—the base of his empire. The surrounding villages were governed from Politschka, which had its own authority. For this reason, in the center of the city, on the town square—instead of a castle—is the impressive town hall. The message conveyed by the magnificent building could not be misunderstood: the nobility thus demonstrated its omnipresence and power to control the disposition of the land. From the perspective of the mostly ground-floor city dwellers, the towering building was a vivid reminder of the hierarchical social structure. They worked down here for those who ruled up there. Above all, a look at the second quarter of the 18th century shows the generosity and artistic wisdom of the city lords. The prosperous economy had indeed given the city, at a time that was also marked by ups and downs, a "Golden Age", an age that still fascinates us today and raises the question of whether it will be possible again in this form. At that time, there was no hesitation in devoting considerable funds to extensive artistic endeavours, the results of which are still visible today. It is expressed in the successful harmony of the urban planning concept, in the architecture, sculpture, painting, and crafts still to be found here. The leading expert on the Bohemian Baroque, Ivo Kořán, believes that "this Baroque complex is absolutely exceptional for its time. A small town here has evidently been inspired by the decoration of the leading cities of the kingdom and has presented itself as the cultural centre of the region. The city has used the forms of dynamic Baroque and, in cooperation with Prague and local creators, has produced a well-thought-out, organic complex of construction and sculptures, comparable to the magnificent undertakings of the nobility. The construction of the town hall in the middle of the square and the colossal Obelisk of the Virgin Mary, which surpasses similar monuments in the region in both size and workmanship, are extraordinary. This ennoblement of the city through the construction and the statues is also undoubtedly a manifestation of Catholic orthodoxy in a region that at the time was still deeply steeped in heresy."

Town Hall

Economic prosperity made it possible for the councillors to construct a new, more dignified building that better represented the bustling city than did the old town hall. It was said to have cost as much as the Obelisk of the Virgin Mary, which was estimated at 6,289 guilders. Not in dispute is the high quality of both structures.

In older literature (Zdeněk Wirth and Dobroslav Líbal[2]), Franz Maximilian Kaňka (František Maxmilián Kaňka), appointed imperial architect in 1724, is cited as the lead architect of the palatial town hall. It dominates the town square at its center, and together with the Obelisk of the Virgin Mary and two impressive fountains, forms a thoroughly composed whole, most effectively viewed from its eastern front, when passing through Masaryk Street or Tyrš Street.

In the northwest corner is the Chapel of St. Francis Xavier, which extends over the first two floors. Next to the altar are the statues of St. Ignatius of Loyola and St. Francis of Borja, which, together with St. Francis Xavier, form the triumvirate of Jesuit saints. Reliquaries with relics of St. Francis Xavier and St. Ignatius certainly contributed to the importance of the chapel. Although the Jesuits did not have a seat in Politschka—their nearest college was in Lusche (Luže)—we can assume that the fact that the chapel was dedicated to the Jesuit saints can be interpreted as a determination of the citizens of Politschka to support the missionary work of the Jesuits. After all, many Protestants still lived in their sovereign domain.

Noteworthy is the small crucifixion sculpture in the chapel, which is attributed to Georg F. Patzak and which might have come from the old town hall. The remaining sculptures are probably the work of Franz Patzak (František Pacák), the son of Georg F. Patzak, who had a number of other commissions in Politschka.

The Obelisk of Mary and the Carefully Composed Town Square

The Politschka Square is a thoughtfully composed whole, in the middle of which a town hall has been located since the Middle Ages. In front of the east façade of the old town hall, two fountains were erected in 1727, a little later the Obelisk of the Virgin Mary. In the years from 1733 to 1744 the new town hall was constructed, preserving the tower of the older Gothic building. The square and its components were clearly part of a larger urban planning concept in which aesthetics also played a key role. The Obelisk of the Virgin Mary is visible from all four access roads to the square, and positioned in such a way that it is not obscured by the town hall. These structures are complemented by two symmetrically arranged fountains.

The Obelisk of the Virgin Mary—a plague column—is not only the most important monument of Baroque sculpture in Politschka, but it is also one of the most artistically valuable and monumental works of the Bohemian Baroque. The art historian Vratislav Nejedlý says: "It is hard to find a parallel, even among the works of Matthias Bernhard Braun. Only in a few columns are the dimensions, proportions and compositional gradation from the foundation to the summit so impressively defined and

City Hall,
Politschka (Polička)

Marian Obelisk,
Georg F. Patzak,
Politschka (Polička)

laid out as in the sculptural colossus in Politschka." The Obelisk of the Virgin Mary was erected in 1727–1731 in honor of the Virgin Mary and as a sign of gratitude for the averting of the plague of Politschka in 1713. The architectural composition used to be attributed to Franz Maximilian Kaňka, but recently some specialists tend to consider the sculptor Georg F. Patzak to be the originator of the design. He also sculpted and erected the 22 meter (72 ft)-high monument.

Patzak has masterfully succeeded in creating the dynamic of movement and gesture. Although the group of figures is usually referred to as a column, the basic shape of the plague column is a triangular obelisk, which is architecturally structured at its base and holds figures of saints and angels all over its vertical surface.

The highest group appears to be "shrouded in clouds". The triangular base clearly indicates the Trinity. Around the parterre there is a stepped balustrade, at the corners of the pillars of the obelisk are the statues of St. Joachim (an old man with a stick), and St. Anne (an old woman with a book), who are the parents of the Virgin Mary, as well as St. Joseph, the husband of the Virgin Mary. The iconographic progression begins with the family of the Virgin Mary and her Immaculate Conception and culminates in a statue of Mary, the Immaculate, near Heaven. In this way the artist achieves a unity of salvation history.

The first floor of the new Town Hall is finished dynamically with wavy cornices, and bevelled, decorated corners. Niches are embedded in the walls, in which statues stand on tambour pedestals. Directly opposite the entrance to the town hall, in main line of sight, is the statue of St. Wenceslas (with princely hat and knightly armour), as well as that of St. Vitus (with his rooster) and St. Florian (with water in the tub and a burning house). This floor is probably the

St. Mary Immaculata, Georg F. Patzak, Politschka (Polička)

one dedicated to the patron saints of the country, indicating a national patriotic sentiment. St. Wenceslas was the first and most important patron saint of the country and the "heir of the country". On his chest hangs the Palladium of Bohemia of Old Bunzlau (Stará Boleslav), according to legend a relief of the Virgin Mary with Child Jesus, a symbol of national protection. The incorporation of St. Vitus among the patron saints of the country is probably due to his burial in the Metropolitan Church in Prague, St. Vitus Cathedral. While St. Florian is not one of the patron saints of the country, he protects against conflagrations, so is not a saint to be neglected.

On the cornices of the second floor base are statues of St. Sebastian (pierced by arrows), St. Roch (as a pilgrim with his dog) and St. Charles Borromeo (in cardinal's robe, with crucifix, see p. 35). These were considered patron saints against the plague and were, therefore, of great importance at that time.

On the walls there are three reliefs of the Virgin Mary, which can be clearly identified with inscriptions. Depicted is the relationship of the Virgin

Mary with the three persons of the Trinity, which is mentioned repeatedly. Mary is depicted as a humble servant of the Lord (the scene with God the Father), as the mother of the Son of God (scene with Jesus) and as the bride of the Holy Spirit (scene with the Holy Spirit).

The third floor, not too high, is architecturally structured and closes in a mighty cloud, from which in turn grows a slender, three-sided obelisk, which appears to be enveloped by a cloud and surrounded by angels' heads.

The group of statues culminates in the statue of the Virgin Mary. The obelisk is completed with a three-sided Ionic chapter on which there is a cloud with the globe around which a snake—the devil—winds. It holds in its mouth the apple with which it seduced Eve. Mary, whose purity is indicated by the crescent moon, an ancient symbol of virginity, steps on the serpent with her foot. Her halo is comprised of twelve stars, symbolizing the twelve apostles. The Virgin Mary is depicted as a bareheaded girl with her hands folded in prayer. This type of representation is called Immaculate, that is, the Immaculate in the sense of the Immaculate Conception at birth.

The Baroque statues on the exterior were mostly painted in one color with oil paints, both to imitate a nobler stone and to protect the statue. From the calculations for the white color, we can conclude that the whole obelisk had a whitish color, which was supposed to evoke the impression of marble. The statue at its top was gilded, as were the metal adornments of the saints. The cartouches with the inscriptions were probably dark green. Over the centuries, the paint was renewed several times, and in 1927 was removed to clean the stone, so its current appearance gives a different impression than when the obelisk was first erected.

On the obelisk there is a series of gilded inscriptions:

1. Above the statue of St. Wenceslas:
COLOSSVS
GRATITVDINIS
GLORIÆ
MARIANÆ
VOTIVVS
[Monument dedicated in gratitude to the honor of Mary]. The enlarged (here bolded) letters are also Roman numerals and represent 1731 as a chronogram—the letter *V* must be read as a *U* at the appropriate point.

2. Under the statue of St. Wenceslas:
Sub
faventissimis Auspiciis
Augustissimae et felicissimae Regnantis
Imperatricis
ELISABETHÆ CHRISTINÆ
Dominae Dominae Nostrae Clementissimae
Errectus.

[Erected under the most gracious patronage of the most venerable and auspicious sovereign Empress Elisabeth Christina, our most benevolent mistress].

The city council of Politschka was aware of the uniqueness of the Marian obelisk and thus entered into written contact with Michael Heinrich Rentz, a court engraver of Count Sporck in Kukus (Kuks), probably the most important engraver of his time, commissioning him to make a large copper engraving of the plague column. The city councillors of Politschka had ambitious goals, but Rentz was working at full capacity and apologized in writing for not being able to carry out the order immediately. It was not until 1738 that he sent a drawing for appraisal and asked for the fixed price of 200 guilders for engraving on the plate and another twenty

St. Michael, Georg F. Patzak, Politschka (Polička)

guilders for the purchase of a polished tablet from the coppersmith. At the same time, he promised to deliver it within a period of one year, so that it could be dedicated to Empress Elisabeth Christine on her birthday. In the letter, he praised the quality of the obelisk: "In the whole Kingdom of Bohemia I cannot say where—together with the statue of the Trinity in Teplice—a more magnificent monument could be seen." However, the engraving was not finished and delivered to Politschka until 1742. The dimensions of the plaque are quite extraordinary—111 by 52 cm (44 x 21 inches)—the asking price of a total of 220 guilders was also extraordinarily high. In fact, Georg F. Patzak received only one hundred guilders for the stone statue at the fountain and Ondřej Andršt received the same sum for the picture on the main altar. From the above, it is clear that the city was very interested in promoting as its primary sculptural monument—the obelisk.

Patzak's Wells

The water was fed into the wells by a wooden pipeline from the Troubný pond. The upper fountain was carved by Georg F. Patzak in 1727 for 350 guilders, and the statues for the fountains—St. George for one hundred guilders, St. Michael for another 62 guilders. In the center of the water basin is a pillar crowned by four dolphins that spout water and carry the pedestal of the statue on their upturned tails. We have no information about the origin of the statues. Usually, as with the obelisk, the sandstone was not left in its original color, but it was given a protective monochrome coat of paint, which was supposed to imitate the more expensive white marble. St. Michael steps on the defeated devil and holds a sword in his upright hand and an oval shield with the initials IHS, an abbreviation of the name Jesus in Greek, in his other hand. The Jesuits, to whom Georg F. Patzak was religiously close, made this "sacred monogram" IHS their own coat of

St. John Nepomuk, Georg F. Patzak, Politschka (Polička)

arms and interpreted it as a short form of Iesum Habemus Socium ("We have Jesus as a companion"). In the Western Church, the IHS has taken on an additional meaning: Iesus Hominum Salvator, which means Jesus, Saviour of mankind. Among the initials are three nails from the cross of Christ. St. George kneels on the dragon and plunges the lance into its throat. The usual scheme is varied in Politschka; the dragon is not male, as everywhere else, but female. This is probably due to the fact that the Czech noun for dragon is feminine.

It would be inappropriate to ascribe to the group of statues in the context of iconographic interpretation a meaning that was not yet common at the time of its creation. Since St. George was the patron saint of knights and his popularity had waned with the end of the Middle Ages, it is surprising that he has been given such a prominent place in this regal city. The explanation may be provided by the neighbouring well. The Archangel Michael depicted there defeats the devil, St. George kills the dragon, which, like the devil, is also a symbol of evil. Both statues convey the same message, that of the defeat of evil—or the devil. They stand for the victory of the righteous faith. In an area riddled with heretics (as Protestants were considered), as was Politschka and its environs at that time, this can certainly also be seen as a decision by the city council to displace people of other faiths in their domain.

The Statue of John Nepomuk

Georg F. Patzak also created the statue of John Nepomuk in 1727. The statue stands in front of the southern wall of the town hall on a slender pedestal. John Nepomuk was beatified in 1721—and canonized in 1729. His canonization was accompanied by great celebrations, with his popularity extended not only to the entire Habsburg monarchy, but also to Bavaria.

St. George, Georg F. Patzak, Politschka (Polička)

St. James Church, Politschka (Polička)

The Church of St. James

A signficant change took place in the Church of St. James (Kostel svatého Jakuba) in the first half of the 18th century, mainly under its dean, Karl Nepauer, through the acquisition of the magnificent altars with their rich sculptural and iconographic decoration. The main altar of the Apostle St. James the Elder, (including the statues of St. Wenceslas and St. Vitus), was created in 1752 by Franz Patzak. There was also the altar of the patron saint of the country, St. John of Nepomuk, with the statues of St. Procopius and St. Adalbert made in the years 1736–1738. There, too, is the altar of the "plague saint", Charles Borromeo with the statues of St. Roch and St. Sebastian from those same years, 1736–1738, and in the nave, the altar of the Holy Cross.

It is unclear whether the statues of the Pietà and the Farewell of Christ with the Virgin Mary that have survived to this day are by George F. Patzak or by Franz Patzak—we are more inclined to the authorship of George. In any case, the statues come from the altar of the Holy Cross and not from Calvary, as the older literature indicates. An entry about the pulpit, which has not been preserved, refers to the year 1741: "According to his contract, Mr. Patzak was paid 140 guilders for a new pulpit, masterful work and excellently decorated with the statue depicting the Good Shepherd."

The Calvary around the church was a fascinating work, but with the exception of two angels, it was destroyed during the fire in 1845. Along the southern and eastern outer walls of the church, between the buttress-roofed chapels, Franz Patzak created 52 life-size polychrome wooden statues for the fourteen Stations of the Cross. The Way of the Cross was consecrated in 1748 by Franciscans from Moravian Trübau (Moravská Třebová).

Georg F. Patzak's main work in Politschka, however, is without a doubt the magnificent plague column, as the Marian Obelisk is also called.

St. Mary Farewell to Jesus, Franz Patzak, Chrudim MuBaSa

II.4
Georg F. Patzak in the National Gallery of Prague
(Tomáš Hladík)

In the National Gallery next to Prague Castle, there are only a few examples of the Baroque art of the Patzaks. Among them, however, are three polychrome crucifixion groups, which are among the best works of Patzak. Tomáš Hladík, an expert on the Baroque at the National Gallery, traces its origins and establishes important connections. It is striking that Patzak has taken very original paths in the design of the works of art. They also show how his extraordinary craftsmanship is artistically effective.

1   Translation from Czech: Hana Hadas; Adaptation: Werner Honal
    Translation from German to English and Adaptation: Cynthia Fontayne
2   Zdeněk Wirth, "Soupis památek historických a uměleckých v království Českém od pravěku do počátku XIX. století XXII. Politický okres Poličský", Praha 1906.

Additionally

David Junek – Stanislav Konečný, "Dějiny města Poličky", Polička 2015.
Dobroslav Líbal, Lubomír Reml, "Polička: Historický a architektonický vývoj královského věnného města a okolí", Praha 1961.

Figures under the Cross, Georg F. Patzak, Prague (Praha)

III.

Main Altar,
Georg F. Patzak,
Schmirschitz (Smiřice)

III. Echoes

Josef Tejkl, Königgrätz (Hradec Králové)

In J. Tejkl's "Calvary": G.F. Patzak as a Stage Hero
(Jan Císař)

The theatre critic Jan Císař describes how Josef Tejkl's play "Stone against the Scythe (Kosou na kameni)" became the play "Calvary". In a drama with great tension upon tension, the main character of the piece, the sculptor and woodcarver Georg F. Patzak, searches for himself and his place in the world of art, rebelling against the authorities and destiny itself. The State security (Czech: Státní bezpečnost, StB for short), quickly realized that the parable "Artists vs. Ecclesiastical Authority" was directed against the repression by the communist government of Czechoslovakia. Only the play's nomination for the prestigious Alfred Radok Prize and the Velvet Revolution of 1989 made the performance possible.

Calvary Cross,
Georg F. Patzak,
Prague (Praha)

J. Roubinek,
Königgrätz (Hradec Králové)

G. F. Patzak / J. F. Pacák on Stage
(Vojtech Berger)

In this essay, Prague journalist Vojtech Berger recounts how in 1991 he attended a performance of Josef Tejkl's play "Calvary" on the Kulm (Chlumek) in Lusche (Luže). It is intended to better acquaint the public with the main character of the piece, Georg F. Patzak, the great sculptor of the Baroque period. For this purpose, the play returned to the main scene of the parable-like conflict between his Jesuit superior with the conservative religious ideas and the free artistic ideas of the sculptor Patzak. It was on behalf of the Jesuits that Patzak had decorated the interior of the Maria-Hilf-Kirche on the Kulm. The play's action shows not only the resistance of the artist but also how easily the masses can be manipulated into taking the side of an oppressive regime. Although Vojtech Berger was not able to interview Josef Tejkl, who died in a mountaineering accident in 2009, he was able to interview others involved, such as Jiří (Georg) Roubínek, the amateur actor who portrayed Georg F. Patzak in the play.

V. V. Štech is Imprisoned in Dachau and Buchenwald during the Nazi's "Albrecht I" Campaign
(Werner Honal)

Immediately after the proclamation of the Nazi protectorate in 1939, the Gestapo launched the so-called "Operation Albrecht I" in the Prague area, intended to eliminate persons who could organize an expected Czech resistance against the German occupation. Among those targeted were supporters of Czech autonomy and anti-fascist intellectuals such as the art historian and Baroque expert Václav Vilém Štech. Štech came to the attention of the Nazis because he referred to aspects of the Baroque as "Czech", not "Bohemian" or "German". He also transformed the names of East Bohemia residents Georg Patzak and his son Franz Patzak into Czech, Jiří and Frantisek Pacák, without referring to their German names. At the beginning of WWII he was arrested, and survived imprisonment first in the concentration camp at Dachau and then until 1942 in Buchenwald.

V.V. Štech, bust, Prague (Praha)

Štech goes to the KZ (Concentration Camp), Document, Prague (Praha)

IV.

St. Franz Xaver.
Josef or Georg F. Patzak
Schurz (Žireč)

A Journey Through East Bohemia and Experiencing the Works of Baroque Sculptors Patzak (Pacák)

(Vojtech Berger)

So near and yet so unknown:

Politschka (Polička)—Königgrätz (Hradec Králové)—Elbe Valley (údolí Labe)—Giant Mountains (Krkonoše).

From Prague (Praha) to the Elbe Valley and the Bohemian-Moravian High Plateau ⋯>

1 Chrudim

537 01 Chrudim
Population: 23000
Elevation: 240 m (788 ft)
A 13th century royal city
17th century pilgrimage site
19th century industrial town
12 km (7 mi) south of Pardubitz (Pardubice)
Pardubický kraj (region Pardubitz)
Okres (district) Chrudim
www.chrudim.eu

It takes an hour and a half by car to go east from Prague to Chrudim. Shortly after the motorway ends at Pardubitz, the city skyline appears on the horizon, although not one that is particularly inviting, as it appears dominated by prefabricated and industrial buildings. But two church towers reassure the visitor that Chrudim is also a valuable historical town center, once dubbed the "Athens of East Bohemia". The information center directly on the church square is open weekdays and Saturdays, and offers materials in Czech and German about the town's most important sights.

In the small area around the parish church of the Assumption of the Virgin Mary, you will find several jewels of Baroque art. In the church itself, it is the altar by Georg F. Patzak. If you come here in the summer (June–September), the church is open every day except Monday, between 9 a.m. and 5 p.m., and you will meet someone who will provide information about the church in Czech. In other months, a visit to the church is possible after consultation with the parish office. More information, including times of church services, can be found at www.farnost-chrudim.cz.

Directly in front of the church stands the 18-meter (60 feet) tall column of The Transfiguration of the Lord (also known as the Marian or Plague Column), which incorporates the work of several Baroque artists.

An absolute must for every Chrudim visitor who is interested in Baroque art is the MuBaSo, the Museum of Baroque Statues. Opened in 2011, this unique space is located in the former St. Joseph's Church, just a few steps away from the main square. Among the exhibits are three wooden figures attributed to Georg F. Patzak and his son Franz. From April to October, it is open daily between 9 a.m. and 5 p.m.; in winter, only on weekends and holidays. Audio guides are available in Czech and German. The MuBaSo is definitely worth seeing, as is the rest of the historical city center and its magnificent houses.

MuBaSo, Chrudim

Column of Transfiguration
J. P. Čechpauer, Chrudim

St. Tobias,
Georg F. Patzak, Lusche (Luže)

2 Lusche (Luže)

538 54 Luže
Population: 2500
Elevation: 309 m (1,013 ft)
1141—First documentary mention
1690 to 1773—owned by the Jesuits
2007—City charter
Pardubický kraj (region Pardubitz)
Okres (district) Chrudim
www.luze.cz

Landscape at Lusche, Lusche (Luže)

The small village of Lusche is located halfway between Chrudim and Politschka (Polička), about half an hour's drive from either. On the approach by car, the monumental pilgrimage church of Mariahilf (Mary's Help) appears suddenly around a curve. The surprising discrepancy between the size of the church and that of the village increases the closer and higher one goes. In Lusche, the Baroque builders skillfully blended the architecture with the landscape. The church towers over the whole area not only because of its size, but also because it stands high on a hill, the Kulm (Chlumek).

In recent years more than 60 million crowns has been invested in renovating the church, both outside and inside, for the first time in 80 years. The sacristan takes great pride in the now gleaming building and is quick to point out a group of wooden figures, pulpit and the main altar. "They're from Patzak....". Indeed, the signature of Georg F. Patzak can be found on all these works, and the whole church is influenced by his style. His work there, which spanned a decade beginning in 1701, was so exceptional that the Jesuits released him from serfdom. The sculptor and Jesuit brother Franz Baugut (1668–1726), who worked in Kuttenberg (Kutná Hora) from 1709, and his companions Jan Kostelník and Maximilian Brabenc also worked there and certainly had an influence on Patzak's freedom and his artistic work.

The church complex's infrastructure is covenient for tourists and pilgrims, including an elevator for those who cannot manage the steep stairs and a screen offering information in eight languages. Tens of thousands come each year. Some pilgrimage days have been given nicknames, e.g. cherry pilgrimage, cucumber pilgrimage, and plum pilgrimage. Unlike most pilgrimage churches, there are no votive offerings. Fr. Josef Hubálek explains that the communist regime wanted to eliminate all traces of piety among the population. Now the Bishop of Königgrätz is proud of the fact that many pilgrims are coming again.

Although individual visits can be arranged through the parish office, the best way to get inside the church is to attend the service. Also worth a visit are the synagogue in Lusche with the Jewish cemetery and the nearby Košumberk Castle. Full information can be found at www.chlumek.net and at the information center in the village.

St. Josef, Georg F. Patzak, Lusche (Luže)

3 Politschka (Polička)

538 54 Polička
Population: 9000
Elevation: 555 m (1821 ft)
Ring-shaped fortification
12th century—first documentary mention
1307—royal city
1613—destructive fire
Pardubický kraj (region Pardubitz)
Okres Svitavy (district Zwittau)
www.policka.org

St. George and Townhall, Georg F. Patzak, Politschka (Polička)

Once you leave Lusche behind and go towards Politschka, the scenery will change rapidly. Lusche is just at the boundary between the Elbe Lowlands and the Bohemian-Moravian Heights. The farther you go towards the southeast, the hillier the landscape becomes. A brief stop at Village New Castle (obec Nové Hrady) www.obecnovehrady.cz to see Patzak's St. John of Nepomuk also is worthwhile. In this small village, the group of figurines "Oratory of Saint John" (Svatojánské oratorium), by Georg F. Patzak, is standing beside the Baroque Church of Saint James (services on Sunday at 09:30 am). From April to October, you can also visit the Rococo castle and English garden at New Castle. In 2016, the castle was incorporated into the program of the Baroque Days of Leitomischl festival, (detailed in the section on Leitomischl).

Politschka centuries ago attracted some of the best artists of that time, as is clearly evident in its main square. Beside the town hall, you can see the obelisk Marian Column, (also called the Plague Column), last renovated in 2016–2017, a masterpiece by Georg F. Patzak. The figures on the statue can also be seen as miniatures in the nearby town museum (www.cbmpolicka.cz/en). Patzak's personal handwriting also can be found on the two fountains with St. George and St. Michael on the main square and the John of Nepomuk Statue in front of the town hall. The museum offers guided tours in English and German, by appointment.

The guide will also take you to the town hall and its chapel. There you can see a wooden sculpture of the Calvary by Georg F. Patzak. The entry to the chapel is decorated by a torso of "the Crying Angel", an older work by Franz Patzak. There are still remnants of one Station of the Cross beside the St. James Church, the other stations having been destroyed by fire in 1845. Some of the Baroque figures were lent to the Museum of the Baroque at Chrudim on a long-term basis. The church tower is worth a visit, to see the tiny flat where the guard and his family lived. His youngest son grew up to be the world-famous composer Bohuslav Martinu, about whom more can be learned at the town museum.

Information is also available at the municipal information center on the main square (www.ic.policka.org/).

St. John Nepomuk, Georg F. Patzak, Politschka (Polička)

St. Michael and Oblisk,
Georg F. Patzak,
Politschka (Polička)

Rosary Madonna, Franz Patzak, Unter Aujezd (Dolní Újezd)

4 Unter Aujezd (Dolní Újezd)

569 61 Dolní Újezd u Litomyšle
Population: 1974
Elevation: 505 m (1,657 ft)
1167—First documentary mention
1785—There were 251 houses
1928—Great Fire of 21 March
Pardubický kraj (region Pardubitz)
Okres Svitavy (district Zwittau)
www.dolniujezd.cz

Angel at St. Mary, Franz Patzak, Unter Aujezd

The onward journey to Leitomischl could be made via the village of Lower Aujezd (Dolní Újezd u Litomyšle), 13 km (8 miles) to the north. Standing at the intersection by the fire station (GPS 49.82816 N, 16.25671 E), is a sculpture of the Virgin Mary with the baby Jesus in her arms, handing an angel a wreath of roses. The statue is known as the Madonna of the Rosary Shtatul, "Shtatul" being a portmanteau of the Czech word "socha" and the German word "statue". The statue, a gift of the Brotherhood of the Rosary, was created in 1737 by Franz Patzak (František Pacák) when he was just 24. The sculptor, who was also known as Wenceslas F. Patzak (Václav František), was born in 1713 in Lusche, and was the son of the Baroque master Georg F. Patzak.

Then it's just another 11 km (7 miles), about ten minutes, farther north to reach Leitomischl, the region's top destination. ··>

5 Leitomischl (Litomyšl)

570 01 Litomyšl
Population: 10200
Elevation: 330 m (1083 ft)
981—First documentary mention
1259—Market law and court charter established
1344-1554—Diocese of Leitomischl
since 1649—Trauttmansdorff
The Castle is a UNESCO World Heritage Site
Pardubický kraj (region Pardubitz)
Okres Svitavy (district Zwickau)
www.litomysl.cz

Jesus the Good Shepherd, Franz Patzak, Leitomischl

Leitomischl has experienced a true rebirth. Just 25 years ago, the facades of the historic buildings were gray and neglected. Today, Leitomischl is a UNESCO World Heritage site, attracting global awareness and visitors. Old buildings now blend with the latest architectural trends (as seen in the completion of the Piarist College near the City Palace), meriting the city motto, "a historical-modern city".

The city is also known as the birthplace of the composer Bedřich Smetana, who gives his name to a popular festival of classical music, Smetanova Litomyšl. The Baroque period had a very strong influence on the cityscape, not least thanks to the workshop of Matthias Bernard Braun, the Baroque master who was active here. The two main churches in the city have names associated with the Holy Cross. In the Church of the Exaltation of the Holy Cross, the Gothic still has the upper hand, but there are some Baroque jewels to be found, including some wood carvings by Georg F. Patzak. You'll need to go to the provost's office next door to request entry and a guided tour. An advance application is encouraged; details, as well as the schedule for church services, can be found online at www.farnostlitomysl.cz .
The Piarist Church of the Finding of the Holy Cross is a testament to that city motto, "modern-historical". The church still serves its sacred purpose, but also is used as a concert hall, exhibition space and meeting venue. The church itself is a jewel of the Baroque period. The front of the church is decorated with statues of the two patron saints, St. Wenceslas and St. Procopius, created by George F. Patzak in M. B. Braun's workshop. You can get close to them thanks to an observation deck, which has been accessible to visitors since the reopening of the church in 2015. Patzak's female figures on the

balustrade, embodying faith and hope, are also impressive. Much also has changed inside the church. At the upper ambulatory, there is a new exhibition of Baroque statues and wooden figures. The two parts of the exhibit space are connected by a new bridge over the transept. Over and over the name Patzak appears throughout the church; both son Franz and father Georg worked for a long time on the design and decoration of the interior. Currently, the side altars created by Georg F. Patzak are in storage awaiting restoration. The new interior includes an artistic light installation, best appreciated after dark. To that end, during the summer, the opening hours of the church are extended until late at night. From May to September, the church is open every day. Out of season you can also arrange an individual viewing. Details and schedules of upcoming events can be found online at www.zamecke-navrsi.cz/piaristicky_chram . Every August, Leitomischl hosts Baroque Days, a week-long festival that celebrates Baroque music, architecture and landscaping, with concerts, pilgrimages and guided tours of historic buildings. The information center at Smetanovo náměstí is a good starting place for visitors. In summer, there is a second information office inside the castle. Details at www.ticlitomysl.cz

The castle garden is open all year round, from early morning to late afternoon.

While the lower part of the garden has been redesigned in the form of an English park, the upper part combines all architectural styles, from Renaissance to Empire.

The Baroque is represented by statues of the gods sculpted by Georg F. Patzak.

Diana,
Georg F. Patzak,
Leitomischl (Litomyšl)

The Faith,
Georg F. Patzak,
Leitomischl (Litomyšl)

6 Moravian Trübau (Moravská Třebová)

Moravian Trübau / Mährisch Trübau
571 01 Moravská Třebová
Population: 10000
Elevation: 360 m (1181 ft)
Renaissance portal, castle, town hall and town center
1257—Founded
1840—Destructive fire
Okres Svitavy (district Zwickau)
Pardubický kraj (region Pardubitz)
www.moravskatrebova.cz

"Small but nice" is a phrase that could describe all the Patzak locations on the itinerary so far, and the town of Moravian Trübau is no different. The easternmost point on the "Patzak map" of East Bohemia is about 35 kilometers (22 miles) away from Politschka or Leitomischl. In the Patzaks' times this would require a full-day trip, but today it's just a short detour. Georg Patzak died here in 1742, but following in his footsteps can still lead visitors to wonderful discoveries. The historic city center shines as in centuries before, with a Renaissance castle, main square and the Stations of the Cross, crowned with a group of Calvary figures, which is a distinctive city landmark and an important work by Patzak and the students in his workshop. Freely accessible, the complex includes the church, cemetery and four Baroque chapels, with views of the surrounding countryside.

The city also strives to convey history in a modern way: not far from the castle stands the so-called Time Gate, an artistic installation that marks the transition between Renaissance and Baroque, a short tunnel that connects the structural elements of both eras. In this way, every visitor can make the transition between "experiences" of the two styles for themselves.

Calvary, Georg F. Patzak,
Moravian Trübau
(Moravská Třebová)

The Time Gate is located on the thematic tourist trail, which leads visitors around to the town's most important sights.
Information, in Czech and German, can be found online at www.moravskatrebova.cz/de/der-tourist. While there, visitors can consult the information center, located directly on the main square in the city.

From Hradec Králové towards the Giant Mountains and Poland ··>

Main Altar
Georg F. Patzak,
Smirschitz (Smirice)

7 Smirschitz (Smiřice)

Smirschitz
503 03 Smiřice
Population: 2900
Elevation: 240 m (787 ft)
1659—Town developed
1711—Baroque chapel built
Today famous for concerts and music programs
Kraj Královéhradecký (region Königgrätz)
Okres Hradec Králové (district Königgrätz)
www.mestosmirice.cz

St. Joachim, Georg F. Patzak, Smirschitz

For more than thirty years, the Königgrätz (Hradec Králové)—Trautenau (Trutnov) route has been being turned into a major highway. Upon completion, it is hoped that it will include the traditional brown and white signs that direct motorists to tourist attractions throughout Europe, because there should be quite a few on this section of the road. The first in the direction of the Giant Mountains (Krkonoše), should bear the name Smiřice, with an image of the Baroque castle and above all, the castle's Chapel of the Epiphany, designed by the best architects working in Bohemia at that time—Christoph Dientzenhofer or Johann Blasius Santini (there is still uncertainty among researchers).

The list of artists who participated in the design of the interior is also impressive. As an example, the main altar with a painting by Johann Peter (Jan Petr) Brandl and sculptured figures by Georg F. Patzak.

The chapel, which is barrier-free, is considered a cultural center with a focus on Baroque music and art. Every year in spring, the "Smiřické svátky hudby" festival celebrates classical music, with performances in the chapel. At other times, there are guided tours for visitors.

Information about the current dates can be obtained from the municipal office in Smiřice: +420 602 316 525, email: infocentrum@mestosmirice.cz.

8 Josefstadt (Josefov Fortress)

551 01 Jaroměř
Population: 12500
Elevation: 254 m (833 ft)
1126—First documentary mention
ca. 1300—City built
1948—City united with the Josefstadt Fortress
Kraj Královéhradecký (region Königgrätz)
Okres (district) Náchod
www.pevnostjosefov.cz

Josefstadt (Josefov), Postcard circa 1930

Let's make a stopover at Jermer (Jaroměř), only a few kilometers from Smirschitz to the north, for another way to experience Baroque art and architecture. Located here is the unique Josefstadt Fortress, which dates from the second half of the 18th century. The huge complex includes kilometers of underground corridors, bastions and military buildings, which fascinate filmmakers and tourists alike. For many years, the city has been looking for investors to bring the billions of Czech crowns necessary for restoration projects. A visit in summer is most popular but winter tours also are possible. You can get information in several languages at the city's cultural center (www.divadlojaromer.cz/kontakt).

Emperor Joseph II, Standard Model, Josefstadt (Pevnost Josefov)

The village of Josefstadt / Josefov is named for Emperor Joseph II (1741–1790). His statue stands on the Riegerplatz (Riegrovo náměstí) in the town center and holds a scroll in his hand with the German text "Abolition of Serfdom" (1781). The statue is a generic figure created by an unknown artist at the former Gräflich Salm'sche art foundry in Blanz (Blansko). It was created in 1793, removed in 1923, and then re-installed on July 7, 1991, to mark the Emperor's 250th birthday.

Vices of Lust, Matthias B. Braun and Georg F. Patzak, Kukus (Kuks)

9 Kukus (Kuks)

544 43 Kuks
Population: 270
Elevation: 283 m (928 ft)
Baroque complex developed since the end of the 17th century.
Kraj Královéhradecký (region Königgrätz)
Okres Trutnov (district Trautenau)
http://www.zkuskuks.cz/

Location Kukus, Kukus (Kuks)

The landscape north of Königgrätz is not particularly spectacular. The country is flat, there are few forests, the journey could soon get boring. But it doesn't last long—the view from the window soon changes. Suddenly, something unexpected appears. It's not your usual castle or palace silhouette. It's different. Without towers, not particularly dominant. But in any case, eye-catching. But since the view soon disappears behind a barrier of houses and trees, you're quickly tempted to leave the main road and take a closer look at the whole thing. You should definitely succumb to temptation. After all, the current tourism slogan is "Zkus Kuks" (www.zkuskuks.cz). A Czech play on words, which translates as "Try Kukus". It's indeed worth trying. Even if Kukus is mainly considered as a destination for the summer season, an inquiry about possible trips for the winter can always be made at the information center www.revitalizacekuks.cz/de or www.hospital-kuks.cz/cs/informace-pro-navstevniky/kontakt.
If you park the car in the large parking lot, you only see what is so tempting at first glance—the view that you saw while driving. In Kukus, the artists have taken advantage of all the possibilities that the landscape here offers, the valley of the young Elbe with a small ridge on both sides. The architects did not drive the building upwards, but horizontally. And it wasn't a mistake: a short path leads down over cascade stairs with a waterfall to the banks of the Elbe and then back up the mountain to the hospital. For some years now, the small community of Kukus is once again the tourist hit of the whole

region. It wasn't always like this. Kukus about twenty years ago was different. There was hardly any infrastructure. On the banks of the Elbe there was a small pub "U Prďoly". The nickname Prďola (hardly translatable) belonged to the long-time innkeeper, who for decades in the same place, and by his peculiar humor and his specialty—beef tartare—became known throughout the region. When the pub was under threat to be replaced by the planned redevelopment of the area, local residents demonstrated for the restaurant to be retained. "Prďola" (actually the innkeeper's name was Jaroslav Vohradník) was one of the few Czech country innkeepers with their own Wikipedia entry.

Today there is no Prďola and no pub left. The house where the bar was located is now completely renovated as a modern restaurant, with the appropriate name of "Baroque". This change in gastronomy is one symbol of a new beginning for the whole place. Since 2015 there is another Kukus, almost completely renewed, and with similar ambitions as when it was first developed during the Baroque period 350 years ago—to become an international hotspot for visitors and culture.

Striking at the top of the fortress is the row of figures of virtues and vices, which are definitely worth taking a closer look at. In the monograph *Matthias Bernhard Braun*, the Czech art historian Emanuel Poche and his pupil Ivo Kořan write that in Matthias B. Braun's workshop it was Georg F. Patzak who was the creator of certain figures. These are the figures of chastity, sincerity and industry in the series of virtues and the figures of envy, lust, gluttony, of sloth, despair and guile from the series of vices.

"The clearest characteristic ... and proof of Patzak's cooperation is the idiosyncratic design of the drapery of these figures." (p. 106). "The outlines of the curves and wrinkles are caused by the wide use of the chisel, giving the drapery a certain stiffness and a decidedly carved angularity. Viewed from a distance, we have a cascade of levels here, which intersect and overlap once, and then again in soft contrasts light and shadow, flickering to differentiate." (p. 107)

Major external changes can already be seen on the way to Kukus. For some time now, there is a direct bicycle path from Königgrätz that ends in Kukus. An extension towards the Giant Mountains is planned. Upon discovery of the Kukus environment, every visitor is faced with a choice. Four wheels or two? Or none at all? The one who chooses walking can see much more in the area. By bike, you can reach about eighty percent of the Baroque landscape, by car significantly less. Speaking of how to get there: the planned motorway was to pass very close to Kukus. Will the historical spirit of the place be lost as a result? Hopefully not, because there should be no direct view from the hospital to the motorway. But the new road will be only a few hundred meters away. An impact on the atmosphere in the entire area is therefore probably unavoidable. It remains to be seen.

What makes Kukus special is not only the hospital itself, with all the magnificent statues and buildings. Rather, it's the almost realized idea of turning a common Bohemian countryside into a Baroque garden. That is, the landscape as a whole, and thus also the respective works of art and buildings in the landscape.

To understand this, you should follow the yellow marked tourist path. It leads from the hospital to the nearby forest, where a relief of St. Francis is carved into a rock. There is also a spring nearby; it's a beautiful, almost secret place. From there, the path continues, and in about an hour at the latest you will reach M. B. Braun's Bethlehem Sculpture Park and its Nativity scene. In the middle of the forest are these high-profile examples of the Baroque in Bohemia.

Vices of Gluttony,
Matthias B. Braun and
Georg F. Patzak, Kukus (Kuks)

10 Braun's Bethlehem Sculpture Park (Betlém, Nativity Scene)

Bethlehem (Kukus) is Part of Stangendorf (Stanovice u Kuksu)
544 01 Stanovice u Kuksu, Dvůr Králové nad Labem
Population: 0
Elevation: 272 m (892 ft)
Kraj Královéhradecký (region Königgrätz)
Okres Trutnov (district Trautenau)
www.braunuvbetlem.cz/de/braunuv-betlem

For many years, preservationists have been arguing about how these works from Braun's workshop have been preserved. The unique outdoor figures have been badly damaged by various culprits including acid rain, the growth of wet forest moss, and vandalism. This stands in stark contrast to the works in nearby Kukus, where millions of euros have been spent on preservation. While the splendor of Braun's Bethlehem may have faded, the magical atmosphere of this remote place remains. In recent years, wayfinding signage has improved considerably, and a new nature trail is enhanced with interpretation panels showing what the area looked like in Baroque times, which was quite different. Where today you can only see a dense forest, a Way of the Cross once led up from the village of Schurz (Žireč). There were chapels, hermitages, springs, even a vegetable garden in the forest. The research seeks to confirm who worked in M.B. Braun's workshop at that time. In addition to his nephew Anton Braun,

The Three Kings, Matthias B. Braun and Georg F. Patzak, Kukus (Kuks)

it also might have been Josef Patzak or Georg F. Patzak who may have designed for Braun a number of the figures of virtues and vices in Kukus.

Even the experts admit that Braun's Bethlehem is slowly sinking; the process can be slowed down, but not stopped. However, there are signs that the place can live on spiritually, even in the 21st century. On the one hand, an active citizens' association has been founded in Dvůr Králové nad Labem, (Königinhof a.d. Elbe), which is creating pressure to finally do something. On the other hand, since 2008 there has been a new, modern Way of the Cross installed at the base of the forest. It is in no way reminiscent of the Baroque statues that stand a few hundred meters away. However, it does not interfere with the genius loci, its "spirit of place", and also uses sandstone, the traditional material of East Bohemia. At the end of the 19th century, only 20 kilometers (12 miles) from here, in the small town of Horschitz (Hořice), a technical school for sculptors was founded, at that time the only institution of its kind in Central Europe. The school still exists, and the students there work with this same stone as the Baroque masters once did.

St. John Nepomuk,
Georg F. Patzak,
Schurz (Žireč)

11 Schurz (Žireč)

544 04 Žireč
Population: 450
Elevation: 278 m (912 ft)
1348: first documented mention
Baroque castle with church
Herb garden and park
Since 1964—part of Königinhof on the Elbe
Kraj Královéhradecký (region Königgrätz)
Okres Trutnov (district Trautenau)
www.barokniarealzirec.cz

Baptism by St. Franz Xaver, Georg F. Patzak, Schurz

St. Florian, Georg F. Patzak, Schurz

A few years ago, the list of tourist destinations in this area would have ended here. The village of Schurz is only a stone's throw away from Braun's Bethlehem, but in the 20th century it was only perceived as a crossroads on the way to Kukus, and not as a destination itself. Today it is, especially in the summer season. The castle in Schurz is not the usual tourist attraction. The entire building, including the church and park, has been renovated and is now partially accessible to visitors. From April to October, you can visit the herb garden and buy various local products offered there. Herb cultivation only resumed here in 2013, but the tradition goes back to the times when neighboring Kukus was at the peak of its fame and when the Jesuits ruled in Schurz.

The Baroque castle church of St. Anna is also remarkable. Not only because of the portal created by Georg F. Patzak, but also the exquisite interior where he appears again among the creators of the figures, an example being the beautiful polychrome wooden statue of Maria Immaculate (see chapter I.3), which he created around 1725 and which today is on loan to an exhibition at the Museum of Baroque Sculptures in Chrudim (www.mubaso.cz). Another unique feature of the church is a Baroque carillon with keyboard, dating to the 18th century, which is still played on special occasions. The church is accessible in the summer season, but not daily. The possibility of a guided tour of the church, herb garden and accessible areas of the castle can be made by telephone arrangement (www.zamekzirec.cz/navstevni_doba.php).

Also of note are in front of the church the statue of St. John Nepomuk and the statue of St. Francis Xaver on the Schurzer Mühlberg (see chapter I.1) on the way to Rennzähn (Zboží) and St. Florian on the way from Schurz to Stangendorf (Stanovice), in the direction of Kukus, all by Georg F. Patzak, figures that the artist designed to be part of the landscape. With the hilly areas of the Elbe, this terrain is unique in Europe.

Main Altar, Georg F. Patzak, Dubenetz (Dubenec)

12 Dubenetz (Dubenec)

544 55 Dubenec
Population: 660
Elevation: 296 m (971 ft)
1229—first documented mention
1343—Church of St. Josef erected in the Gothic style
1623—Purchase by Albrecht from Waldstein
1662—Sold to the Jesuits in Schurz / Žireč
1736 and 1740—St. Josef redesigned in Baroque style
Kraj Královéhradecký (region Königgrätz)
Okres Trutnov (district Trautenau)
www.dubenec.cz

St. Josef Church, Dubenetz (Dubenec)

The difficulty in reviving historical heritage sites can be seen in Dubenetz, another small town nearby. At first glance, the Baroque church of St. Joseph seems to be far too big for such a small, remote village. The exterior presents a matte façade, but inside you could admire what is probably the last and one of the most valuable works by Georg F. Patzak. Unfortunately, the church is usually closed, its last pastor having departed in 1989, and no parish services are scheduled there. The old vicarage remains and stands right next to the church, which only emphasizes the contrast between the current states of the two buildings. The vicarage has been carefully renovated, with respect for the original Baroque style, under the supervision of preservationists, and converted into a guesthouse. The current operators are willing to open the church to interested parties by telephone arrangement. The guesthouse can be a good starting point for excursions in the area (www.penzionnafare.cz/de/kontakt). Kukus and Dubenetz are only a few kilometres apart but worlds apart in its heritage status. Kukus seeks to be a national attraction of the arts, while Dubenetz struggles to save the church of St. Joseph, which houses the last work of Georg F. Patzak.

And further into the Giant Mountains ··›

Why go to the Giant Mountains? For hiking? Sure. For skiing? Of course! Nature, gastronomy, wellness—, in all these areas, the highest Czech mountain range has taken a big step forward over the last 25 years. But visitors interested in history and art of the Baroque period will also find places of interest in this region. While the tourism industry has emphasized mountain views and recreation, walks through these small towns with historic churches are equally rewarding to the visitor.

13 Qualisch (Chvaleč)

542 11 Chvaleč
Population: 660
Elevation: 493 m (1617 ft)
1329—First written mention as Qualisdorph
1706—Construction of the Church of James the Elder
1869—Recorded population of 1427, due to textile industry and mining
Kraj Královéhradecký (region Königgrätz)
Okres Trutnov (district Trautenau)
www.chvalec.cz

St. Jakob Church, Qualisch (Chvaleč)

If you enter this place name into your navigation system, e.g. in Berlin, the fastest route to the East Giant Mountains region will probably be calculated through Poland. This shows how the situation has changed over the last 25 years; but especially in the last 75 years. The Second World War and its aftermath permanently changed this area. You can also see it in Qualisch, then as now the center of the region.

The Church of St. James the Elder, built in 1706, is a dominant landmark in Qualisch often seen in old postcards of the area, (www.staretrutnovsko.cz/chvalec-pohlednice.php). In 1836, when Johann Gottfried Sommer and Franz Xavier Maximilian Zippe reported on the town and church in the handbook *The Kingdom of Bohemia*, the village had just 1053 inhabitants. However, the fact that the church was under the rule of the bishop of Hradec Králové and also served four other neighbouring villages explains its size and special furnishings. It could just be one of the many churches with crumbling facades in the former Sudetenland, but its interior, co-designed by Georg F. Patzak, sets it apart. Patzak's work is the Calvary group on the tabernacle of the high altar, which he created from wood in the 1730s. His calling card is a small carving of the Calvary group in the Prague National Gallery in Hradčany (see chapter II.4). As unique as the church's artistic contents are, they are well protected for—and from—visitors, with a grille that allows them to look inside, but nothing more. The church is used only occasionally, for concerts and services.

Location, Qualisch (Chvaleč)

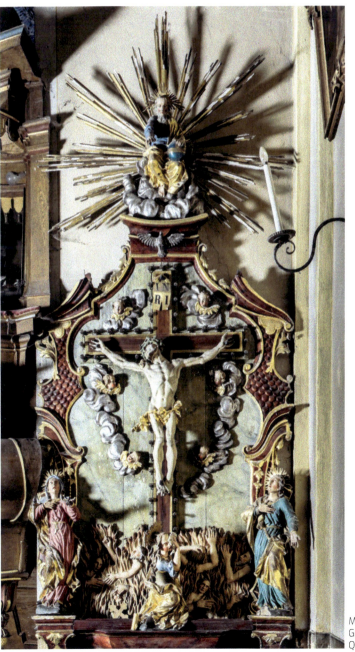

Main Altar, Georg F. Patzak, Qualisch (Chvaleč)

The cemetery next to it speaks to the town's history, with half the gravestones carved with German names and the other half with Czech ones. Qualisch (Qualisdorph in 1329), like almost the entire Czech and Moravian border area, was affected by the expulsion or deportation of the German-speaking population after 1945. In 1930 there were 1145 inhabitants, but in 2016 there were only 660. The cemetery in Qualisch is relatively well maintained and the former citizens come here from time to time. Even though the place is located in a beautiful natural area—the famous sandstone cliffs in Adersbach (Adršpach) are within reach—and a tourism infrastructure has developed, (www.kladskepomezi.cz/en *The Landscape of Stories—Krajina příběhů*), the cemetery in Qualisch is also proof that the area is no longer as lively as it once was. The people responsible for regional tourism and the bishop of Hradec Králové, once the landlord of the church, urgently need to establish access to the works of art in the church. Today, the parish office of Trutnov III—Poříčí in Trautenau (www.bihk.cz/dieceze/trutnov-iii-porici) is locally responsible.

14 Schatzlar (Žaclér)

542 01 Žaclér
Population: 3100
Elevation: 612 m (2008 ft)
1334—Castle built
1795–1992—Coal mining and textile industry
Until 1945—Mostly German inhabitants
Kraj Královéhradecký (region Königgrätz)
Okres Trutnov (district Trautenau)
www.zacler.cz

Holy Trinity Church, Schatzlar (Žaclér)

After World War II and into the 21st century, Schatzlar, a city a half hour's drive north near the Polish border, had to reinvent itself. The many societal changes challenging life there included the end of coal mining in the area and the expulsion of its German inhabitants.

Only about five kilometers (3 miles) south of the city, in Trautenbach (Babí), lies the monumental fortress Stachelberg. Meant to be a fortification against Hitler's army, the construction of its complex of bunkers was interrupted in 1938 by the Munich Agreement. The bunkers are maintained by an association, similar to other monuments of this kind along the northern Czech border. Undoubtedly worth visiting, but "Everyone just comes to the bunker and then drives back," says Inge Salwenderová, the sacristan in Schatzlar. She says that hardly anyone bothers to drive a little further and discover her city.

The Church of the Most Holy Trinity (Kostel Nejsvetejší Trojice) can accommodate at least 250 people, but only about thirty would come to the service, says Salwenderová, herself a Sudeten German. (Her family was not expelled after the war, because her father was too important to the Czechoslovak state as a worker in the coal mine.) The figural decoration of the high altar in the church is one of the most mature works by Georg F. Patzak. It is astonishing how Patzak manages to let the individual groups float freely in the space at this high altar. At the foot of the Trinity—the Holy Spirit as a dove, Christ with the Cross and God the Father—Mary is

Main Altar, Georg F. Patzak, Schatzlar (Žacléř)

Pulpit,
Georg F. Patzak,
Schatzlar (Žacléř)

seated on clouds, flanked by angels. The stone portal on the west side of the church also features sculptures created by Patzak. The eye of God is surrounded by sun rays and clouds with angelic heads. Fruit tendrils hang down from the entablature pieces, which are broken on both sides. The former German residents have twice already financially supported the renovation of the church, and generously so. In 2000, Germans donated one million Czech crowns to the restoration; about 15 years later, money from Germany flowed there again, stimulating further financing from the German-Czech Future Fund. Despite this positive development, the now 72-year-old Salwenderová still feels cause for concern about who will care for the church after her, who will continue to tell its story. But for now, interested visitors can make an appointment, by calling 00420 728 840 260, for a guided tour of the church, with its history presented in the old local German dialect. Should the interior not be accessible, visitors can still admire the opulent main portal also sculpted by Patzak. More information from the parish office can be found at www.bihk.cz/dieceze/zacler/.

Marian Column,
Georg F. Patzak, Schatzlar (Žacléř)

St. Jerome at the Marian Column, Georg F. Patzak, Schatzlar (Žacléř)

Another positive signal for a good reappraisal of history can be found in Schatzlar. On the market square stands the 1725 Marian column, another masterpiece by Georg F. Patzak, erected on behalf of the Jesuit Order. The Schatzlar city information center and an information board are nearby. A 50-page booklet, published by the city in 2015, draws visitors' attention to the small and seemingly insignificant sacred monuments in the area (www.infocentrum-zacler.cz/stahnout-soubor/14.pdf). *History Hidden in the Stone* is the name of the English version. The crosses and statues in the great outdoors prove that the old soul can still be found in the landscape of the Eastern Giant Mountains. "One of the most valuable stone sculptural works in our region" is what Patzak's Marian column is called on page 2 of the booklet. The column has a triangular base, so it is more of an obelisk. Typical of Patzak is the highly moving design of the clothing on the figures. The robe of the slightly spiralling figure of the Virgin Mary on the top of the column, standing on a globe wrapped in a snake and crowned with a wreath of twelve golden stars, looks as if moved by rippling waves. In the foreground is the person of the founder of the Jesuit order, Ignatius of Loyola. Above him is St. Jerome, a bearded old man in a wide-brimmed cardinal's hat with a lion at his feet, which is rarely seen on a Marian column. Also depicted on the column are St. Dominic and St. Bernard. Figures of floating "putti" angels, which also dominate the altar in the church, are found throughout.

Hl. Cross Altar,
Georg F. Patzak,
Hohenelbe (Vrchlabí)

15 Hohenelbe (Vrchlabí)

543 01 Vrchlabí
Population: 12300
Elevation: 477 m (1565 ft)
1359—First documentary mention
1546–1548—Construction
of a moated castle
1705–1725—Establishment
of an Augustinian monastery
1850—Seat of the district administration
until 1945—inhabited mainly by
German Bohemians
Kraj Královéhradecký (region Königgrätz)
Okres Trutnov (district Trautenau)
www.muvrchlabi.cz

Augustinian Church, Hohenelbe (Vrchlabí)

"Gateway to the Giant Mountains"—this description of Hohenelbe is not an exaggeration. From here, all corners of the Giant Mountains are about the same distance away, as the River Elbe emerges from the narrow valley of the high mountains into the foothills.

Its Sudeten German history can be seen, but Hohenelbe looks different from what one expects to see in a "Sudeten city" in the Czech Republic. Everything here has been renovated; even the churches shine. A city for tourists.

In the local museum you can learn a lot about life in the old Giant Mountains, about the beginnings of skiing in Bohemia, and the natural environment. If the weather is bad, you can happily spend an entire day in town. Surprisingly, some of Hohenelbe's fine attractions are not promoted. This is especially true of the Augustinian monastery church, a Baroque masterpiece that's just a five-minute walk from the main square. It is mostly closed to visitors, with the exception of two summer months. So, some advance arrangements are necessary to see the church's artistically most valuable piece, the side altar to the Holy Cross on the right side of the presbytery, which Georg F. Patzak created around 1734. The figure of Mother Mary, marked by the pain of Jesus' death on the cross, is characteristic of G. F. Patzak. The whole altar looks like a theatrical scene, a blue wooden background increases the contrast for the heads of the angels framed by clouds. Under Jesus' left hand, the landscape shows how life springs again from a dry trunk through him. A guided tour of the church in other seasons is theoretically possible, but only on request (www.mestovrchlabi.cz/de). The monastery church is an impressive building, which can be compared with the aforementioned Piarist church in Leitomischl (Litomyšl).

Hohenelbe also has another compelling connection to the Baroque period. It was precisely here in the church that the great art lover and patron, Count Morzin, is buried. The famous composer Antonio Vivaldi has dedicated a collection of concertos to him, including the world-famous "The Four Seasons". Today's city of Hohenelbe also uses this story as a marketing theme and attracts visitors to the church with summer concerts celebrating Vivaldi and other Baroque composers.

There is also some Patzak in the capital of the Czech Republic ··>

16 Prague (Praha)

PSC: 100 00–199 00
Population: 1340000
Elevation: 192 m (630 ft)
50 BC—Settlement of Celtic Boii
until 500 AD—Settlement of the Marcomanni
560 AD—Migration of the peoples: Beginning of the Slavic settlement
~ 850 AD—Construction of the 1st Prague Castle on the Hradschin (Hradčany)
~ 930 AD—Construction of the 2nd Prague Castle (Vyšehrad, Hochburg)
1230/1234—Town charter for Prague
1346—Imperial seat (Charles IV) of the Holy Roman Empire
1348—Foundation of Charles University, 1st university in Central Europe
1350 to 1860—Mostly German-speaking population
1918—Capital of the first free democratic Czechoslovak Republic ČSR
1939 to 1945—Capital of the Protectorate of Bohemia and
Moravia of the German National Socialists
1945—End of World War II and the multilingualism in Prague
1946—Expulsion of the German Bohemians from Prague
1968—Prague Spring "Socialism with a Human Face" crushed
1989—Center of the "Velvet Revolution", overthrow of the communist regime
1993—Capital of the Czech Republic ČR
Kraj (region) Hlavní město Praha (Hauptstadt Prag)
www.praha.eu

It may seem strange to include the Czech capital with small East Bohemian towns and villages during our trip: Prague, the golden city with hundreds of towers, churches and monuments. But it is here that you can find the roots of some of the works that can be admired in Eastern Bohemia today. Georg F. Patzak was born in East Bohemia, which is where he was most artistically active. Today, however, some of his works can also be found in Prague, metaphorical ambassadors for everything he had created in Eastern Bohemia, whetting the visitor's appetite to travel there to seek out more Patzak works.

A city walk can start at the Schwarzenberg Palace on Hradčany, a few meters from Prague Castle. The palace now houses some collections of the National

Calvary,
Georg F. Patzak,
Prague (Praha)

Gallery in Prague, including baroque wooden sculptures by the Patzaks. Dr. Thomaš Hladik, who works there, describes some of them elsewhere in this book (see chapter II.4). The Baroque can certainly be experienced here, even though the palace building itself is considered one of the best examples of the Renaissance in Prague (www.ngprague.cz/en/objekt-detail/schwarzenberg-palace).

Just a few steps away from the palace is a viewing platform, from which a large part of Prague's historic city center can be seen, including the famous Charles Bridge, to which our path continues.

The 30 sculptures that stand on the bridge were created by 14 different artists between 1629 and 1938. We highlight two names. Matthias Bernard Braun (Matyáš Bernard Braun 1684–1738), who was a teacher, collaborator and later a competitor of G. F. Patzak, and Mathias Wenzel Jäckel (Matěj Václav Jäckel 1655–1738), Braun's colleague, a generation older, who had become acquainted with the working methods of Gian Lorenzo Bernini (1598–1680) in Rome and brought them to Bohemia. It is possible that Patzak became familiar with Jäckel's work through the Jesuit College in Kuttenberg (Kutna Hora).

St. Luitgard, Matthias B. Braun , Prague (Praha)

It is best to get a map with all the statues at any information center before entering the bridge, or to look at them online (www.prague.eu/en/object/places/93/charles-bridge-karluv-most). Created by Matthias Bernard Braun are the sculptures of St. Luitgard (counted the 12th on the south side from the old town, with which Braun successfully started his new style in Bohemia in 1710), and those of St. Ivo (1711, 1st south) and those of St. Ludmila (8th south, Braun's late work, 1730). Mathias Wenzel Jäckel created, in 1707, St. Anne with the Child Jesus (4th sculpture on the north side), the Madonna with St. Bernard (1708, 1st sculpture on the north) and the Madonna with St. Dominic and Thomas Aquinas (1708, 2nd sculpture on the north).

In case of bad weather, a visit to the Lapidárium Gallery in the city center is recommended as a substitute for the study of the figures on the Charles Bridge (www.barok.cz). Outside the city center, it is also worth taking a detour to the lapidary of the National Museum in Prague's seventh district, where some original Baroque sculptures are exhibited, (including some by Braun or Jäckel, albeit none of the Patzaks) (www.nm.cz/Hlavni-strana/Visit-Us/Lapidary-of-the-National-Museum.html).

Braun's works are scattered around Prague, in various palaces and Baroque gardens. Braun had a large workshop in Prague whereas Patzak had his in distant Leitomischl. Every Prague tourist walks past Braun's Baroque works; Patzak's Baroque works are located in Eastern Bohemia and visitors are encouraged to visit there as well as the Baroque works in the Prague National Gallery on Hradčany.

Pieta,
Georg F. Patzak,
Prague (Praha)

V. Restoration and Preservation

Commitment to St. Franz Xaver, Josef or Georg F. Patzak, Schurz (Žireč)

Civic Commitment—An Example at Schurz (Žireč). Planted into the Landscape
(Ignác A. Hrdina)

The prime example of a sculpture by Patzak, which was not intended for a church interior, but to be installed in the landscape to inspire it and those who passed by it, is the statue of St. Francis Xavier on the Schurzer Mühlberg. Tradition has it that his outstretched hand holding the cross is pointing to Kukus (Kuks). This is where the Order of St. Hubertus is located, not an ecclesiastical institution but a civilian hunting society. It was founded in 1708 by Count Franz Sporck with his aristocratic hunting friends, ended with his death in 1738, and then revived in November 1989. In 2012, the sculptor Karel Krátký was commissioned to restore this statue, financed with funds from the Order of St. Hubertus, private donations and with the support of the European Union.

Ecclesiastical Commitment—Let the Baroque Works of the Patzaks be Viewed

(Werner H. Honal)

The majority of the Baroque works of art of the Patzak family, wood carvings and stone sculptures can be found in and around churches. As far as they stood inside a church, they were protected from acid rain and other environmental hazards, but most of the time there was no money for timely or proper restoration. For those churches still in use today—although this is not the majority—the episcopal ordinariates do help with expertise and financing ideas. And even if, as in Lusche or Leitomischl (Litomyšl), the restoration is successful, one problem remains: the Patzaks designed their Baroque works of art for the people, not for empty, cordoned-off spaces. Therefore, easy access to the churches containing these works of art must be made possible everywhere. Some good progress has been made in this regard, but more is needed.

Altar St. John Nepomuk,
Franz Patzak,
Leitomischl (Litomyšl)

St. Florian restored,
Georg F. Patzak,
Schurz (Žireč)

An Example of Municipal Commitment: St. Florian and Königinhof on the Elbe River (Dvůr Králové nad Labem)
(Werner H. Honal)

With territorial reform of the administration in 2003, roads far outside the city also came under their jurisdiction, including the road from Schurz (Žireč) to Stangendorf (Stanovice). In order to enliven the landscape, in 1730, the Jesuits from Schurz commissioned Georg F. Patzak to create a statue of St. Florian to be made of sandstone. After the "Velvet Revolution" in Czechoslovakia, in 2014, members of the Order of St. Hubertus, based in Kukus, together with Mr. Josef Mádl Jr. from Stangendorf for the National Institute of Monuments (NPU) uncovered the statue that disappeared behind trees. On the front of the pedestal there is a double cartouche with interesting reliefs of buildings. In 2015, the city council of Königinhof on the Elbe river, the town to which the street now belongs, had the statue restored with the help of regional funding. Once again it is the highlight of the landscape.

℗ Commitment of the Patzak Relatives Alive Today
(Werner H. Honal)

The Baroque sculptors Patzak belonged to the first of about 20 families of this name in the district of Trautenau (Trutnov). Their ancestors, the first Patzak family in Eastern Bohemia, were recruited from Silesia to the foothills of the Giant Mountains around 1450—still without a family name. All of the approximately 2000 out of 2500 Patzaks / Pacák living worldwide who have ancestors in East Bohemia are related to this first Patzak family and thus also to each other. What could these many relatives do to ensure that the masterful Baroque art of the Patzaks, their great contribution to European culture, is further researched, rescued and made accessible to all?

G. F. Patzak comes from the Trautenau area. Many Patzaks still live there today. The city of Trautenau published a book in 2022 *They made Trautenau Famous* (*Proslavili Trutnov*); G. F. Patzak can also be read there.

You can travel to see these works of art, study their splendor, and spread the knowledge of them around the world. The printed and digital publications cited in this book, *Journey in Bohemia's Inspired Landscapes*, also help to achieve this this goal.

Book Presentation, Trautenau (Trutnov)

VI.

Prosperina at Nymphenburg Castle, Dominik Auliczek, Munich (München)

VI Appendices

℞ Bibliography

The books listed in the individual chapters of the Baroque Patzak book *Böhmens beseelte Landschaft* and additional books, especially those about the Baroque sculptors Patzak and their time, are listed here in alphabetical order.

℞ Indices

As a finding aid, there is an index of places and persons in the Baroque Patzak book *Böhmens beseelte Landschaft*.

Credits

The editors Heinz Patzak and Werner H. Honal would like to thank sincerely:
the **authors** Vojtěch Berger, Jan Cisař, Tomáš Hladik, Gerhard Honal, Werner H. Honal, Ignác A. Hrdina, David Junek, Ludmila Kesselgruberová, Ivo Kořán, Marie-Christine Leitgeb, Heinz Patzak, Peter Patzak, Zdenka Paukrtová, Jan Pipek and Stephan Sweerts-Sporck; the **translators** Karel Dolista, Cynthia Fontayne, Hana Hadas; the **graphic designer** Simona Blahutová; the **photographers** Štepán Bartoš, Vojtech Berger, Rudi Handl, Werner H. Honal, Milan Krištof and José Sepp Piños for the images and their publication rights, the Diocese of Königgrätz / Hradec Králové for the approval and **publication rights** to the interior photographs in the churches; the **book design team** Alexander Rendi in cooperation with Eugen Lejeune; the **final proofreaders** Cynthia Fontayne and Peter Patzak; the **lecturer** Gerold Patzak.

We would especially like to thank the **National Monuments Office** (NPU) in Prague, which informed us well about the works of art by the sculptors Patzak. The same applies to the **State Archives** in Trautenau (Trutnov), Königgrätz (Hradec Králové) and the **National Archives in Prague**, which also gave us permission to print photos of important documents (page 44, 45, 46, 47, 71).

Many have often given up an appropriate fee in favor of this non-profit project "Baroque Patzak". God bless you!

Source
Jan Bouček created a comprehensive basis for our work with his **diploma thesis** *Jiří František Pacák a jeho tvorba ve východních Čechách* submitted to the Catholic Theological Faculty of Charles University in Prague in 2015. Many thanks!

Pictures back cover
Georg F. Patzak (1727) St. Nepomuk supported by an angel in Neuschloss (Nové Hrady)
Map for traveling to 16 destinations of Patzaks' art, designed by Simona Blahutova, teacher of graphic design and animation, DUKE high school in Prague

Pictures
Portrait of Dominik Auliczek
(* 1734 in Politschka / Polička; † 1804 in Nymphenburg) painted around 1770 in Munich by Joseph Weiss

Franz Patzak died in 1757 at the age of 43 without descendants of his own. His brother-in-law and student was Dominik Auliczek. He continued the Baroque sculpture of the Patzaks—but not in East Bohemia, where he grew up, but in Munich Nymphenburg. There Auliczek was court sculptor under the Bavarian Elector Max III. Joseph and also model master in the Nymphenburg porcelain manufactory. **The Perl series**, which goes back to him, is still sold today.
For the first time in the history of European porcelain production, in 1793 Auliczek's perl service featured a dodecagonal shape. This Nymphenburg porcelain service is called Perl because the edge is decorated with a string of pearls.

If you take a journey to the Nymphenburg Palace Park in Munich, experience the aftermath of the Baroque sculptor Patzak! (page 49, 119)

D. Dominik Auliczek,
J. Weiss, München (Munich)

From the Perl Series,
Dominik Auliczek,
München (Munich)